Emotionally Durable Design

Objects, Experiences and Empathy

To my wife, Ming Ming

Emotionally Durable Design
Objects, Experiences and Empathy

Jonathan Chapman

publishing for a sustainable future
London • Sterling, VA

First published by Earthscan in the UK and USA in 2005
Reprinted 2006, 2009

Copyright © Jonathan Chapman, 2005

ISBN: 978-1-84407-181-4

Design and typesetting by Safehouse Creative
Printed and bound in the UK by Cromwell Press, Trowbridge
Cover design by Jonathan Chapman

For a full list of publications please contact:

Earthscan
Dunstan House, 14a St Cross Street
London, EC1N 8XA, UK
Tel: +44 (0)20 7841 1930
Fax: +44 (0)20 7242 1474
Email: earthinfo@earthscan.co.uk
Web: **www.earthscan.co.uk**

22883 Quicksilver Drive, Sterling, VA 20166-2012, USA

Earthscan is an imprint of James and James (Science Publishers) Ltd and publishes in
association with the International Institute for Environment and Development

A catalogue record for this book is available from the British Library

Library of Congress Cataloging-in-Publication Data has been applied for

The paper used for this book is FSC-certified.
FSC (the Forest Stewardship Council) is an international
network to promote responsible management of the
world's forests.

contents

CONTENTS

CONTENTS

List of figures

List of acronyms and abbreviations

ABS	Acrylonitrile Butadiene Styrene
AIGA	American Institute of Graphic Arts
C	Celsius
CD	compact disc
CO_2	carbon dioxide
DfX	Design for X
HCI	human–computer interaction
JND	just noticeable difference
LCD	Liquid Crystal Display
LED	light emitting diode
MD	mini disc
MP3	a computer file format that stores a large amount of information in a small amount of space – usually music
NASA	National Aeronautics and Space Administration
NRI	Nomura Research Institute
OECD	Organisation for Economic Co-operation and Development
PC	personal computer
PD	phantile drive
PDA	Personal Digital Assistant
PR	public relations
TB	tuberculosis
VR	virtual reality
VW	Volkswagen

Acknowledgements

I would like to thank the following individuals for their kind support, contributions and comments during the creation of this book:
Ian Lee, John Wood, Nigel Ordish, Beatrice Otto, Sue Anne Lee, Yu-Heng Lu, Rob West and Dr Christian De Groot.

Special thanks are due to the Harold Hyam Wingate Foundation, whose generous scholarship helped to make this project possible, and to photographer Katherine Anne Rose for creating the images featured within this book.

chapter one

the progress illusion

Ecological awakenings

In 1966 the National Aeronautics and Space Administration (NASA) delivered to the world the first photographic images of our planet from outer space, and for the first time in human history we experienced Earth as a holistic and self-supporting organism peacefully suspended in the dark silence of space. We witnessed with our own eyes Earth's protective atmosphere, and were jolted by the evident fragility of this blue gaseous membrane proportionally similar in depth to 'a coat of paint around a football'.[1] The social shockwave that resulted from this uncomplicated revelation gave birth to a new and socially accessible appreciation of the natural environment. The world's largest environmental organization – Friends of the Earth – was founded three years later closely followed by Greenpeace in 1971. From the early 1970s, the output of legislation and transnational environmental policies also grew, placing increasing pressure on designers and manufacturers to improve their standards. Today, public consciousness of the human destruction on the natural world is almost tacit, and few would negate that a dramatic reappraisal of developed world production and consumption methods is imperative: 'proving that the Earth's climate is changing from human actions … is like statistically "proving" the pavement exists after you have jumped out of a 30-storey building. After each floor your analysis would say "so far – so good" and then, at the pavement, all uncertainty is removed.'[2]

Some might refer to the space mission in 1966 as having provided the greatest ecological awakening in modern history. Undoubtedly, it assisted significantly in the societal comprehension of new ecological models and theories, one of these being the Gaia hypothesis – so named after the Greek goddess of Earth, Gaia – which provides an inclusive glance at life on Earth. In Gaia, environmental scientist James Lovelock puts forward the theory that the Earth is a 'tightly coupled process from which the self-regulation of the environment emerges'.[3] His theory, made public in 1968 at a conference regarding the origins of life on Earth, might well be viewed as a logical continuation of Charles Darwin's theories of evolution by natural selection, except that Lovelock classifies animals and inanimate entities within a single category. It also appears to make perfect sense to even the least informed ecologist, making it the popular choice for many. Gaia theory embeds itself within the correlations between all matter on Earth, and in this respect resembles ancient Celtic and other holistic, animistic depictions of human situatedness within nature, quite unlike contemporary ecology with its somewhat anthropocentric tendency to focus chiefly on human-centred endeavours and their environmental impact(s).

Other approaches differ greatly in sentiment to Gaia, such as that of French-born American microbiologist, environmentalist and author Rene Dubos and that of Garret Hardin. Dubos powerfully expresses the concept of humans as *stewards* to life on Earth: in governmental symbiosis with it like supreme gardeners for the entire world. Hardin, on the other hand, a highly trained ecologist and microbiologist, sees humankind as acting out a great tragedy which may not only lead to their own destruction but to that of the whole world. In 1968 he described this theory with great detail in an essay entitled 'The tragedy of the commons'[4] in which he draws comparison between planet Earth and the village common. This analogy is founded on the basis that they are both ecosystems, each of which must live within certain limits – the tragedy being that each villager who uses the common sees only their own impact and never the overall spatial effects of the village population as a whole.

Pressure on resources

Many practitioners claim that our destructive and unsustainable harvesting of this planet's limited reserve of natural resources is due to an escalating human population, founded on the simple premise that more people essentially need more materials to support their existence. This is not actually the case: 'over the last 50 years the world's population has increased by 50 per cent; but our resource utilization has increased by 1000 per cent for the same period'.[5] These statistics demonstrate that increased population is not necessarily exponential with increased resource consumption, as is often assumed. It would be more accurate to say that although an increase in human population will bring an obvious increase in resource consumption, the mess we are in today is more likely to be a result of unsustainable developments in the way we design, manufacture and consume objects in the modern world. It is therefore short sighted to blame the demise of natural resources simply on a rise in population, when it is so evidently not the case.

Pressure and competition for space upon Earth is in constant flux; an ebb and flow of populations, animal, vegetable and mineral wash in and out of space the moment an opportunity arises. The rules of spatial pressure operate in this way by placing 'uneven pressure'[6] on the immediate environment, which forces vast tides of biomass to surge and boil in reaction to the consequent disharmony. As discussed earlier in Gaia, this eternal struggle has always been in progress and always will be. French librarian and writer Georges Bataille, when speaking of pressure, states that any life form will always expand in number or size to fill the space that it has, and only when critical mass has been accomplished will growth level off. He illustrates this theory with the micro-organism duckweed: 'It has a drive to cover any pond with a green film, after which it remains in equilibrium.'[7] The only change likely to occur will happen when an outside factor becomes visible to the equation, such as a tree falling into the pond, or heavy rainfall that doubles the pond's surface area. Life is opportunist and may proliferate under the most obscure circumstances; in the words of Bataille, 'life occupies all available space'.[8]

Owing to the broad range of extreme conditions that can be found on this small planet, most humans – with the obvious exception of hardy scientific researchers – do not actually occupy all available space. Vast expanses of the globe are currently uninhabited due to inhospitable conditions, such as the altitudinal excesses found in the upper Himalayan regions of Nepal or, perhaps, the geological instability of the sulphurous laval plains of the Reykjanes Peninsula in Iceland. However, even in places that are considered to be so inhospitable, there are usually a few well-dressed scientific researchers to be found. For example Vostok, Antarctica, is the home of some of the coldest temperatures recorded on Earth, sometimes reaching a bitter –89° Celsius (C); there is an inhabited Russian research base there, where it is reported that the temperature regularly dips below –60°C. Bataille was right; life is opportunist and endeavours to occupy all available space.

'Human population currently stands at 6.13 billion persons and is growing at 1.33 per cent per year, or an annual net addition of 78 million people.'[9] It is further projected that world population will reach a staggering '8.9 billion in 2050'.[10] According to US Census Bureau estimates:

> World population hit the 6 billion mark in June 1999. This figure is over 3.5 times the size of the Earth's population at the beginning of the 20th century and roughly double its size in 1960. The time required for global population to grow from 5 to 6 billion – 12 years – was shorter than the interval between any of the previous billions.[11]

These statistics demonstrate that the human species is not only growing, but also gathering considerable speed along the way. In a study that Rem Koolhaas – hailed by many as the architect for the new millennium – is conducting with students at Harvard University, it was discovered that the city of Shenzhen near Hong Kong is growing at a rate of 2 square kilometres per year: at 'this pace an architect can afford only two days to design an entire skyscraper'.[12] Although, as Bataille states, population growth alone is not a problem for planet Earth, there are vast expanses of uninhabited land that excess population could spread to. However, the growth of a species whose presence has negative impacts on all other life must be seen as a potential ecological crisis. Excess pressure on resources is one of the lamentable side effects of overpopulation.

We lead a resource-hungry existence, taking out a great deal more from the Earth than we put back in:

> Even bearing in mind a very loose definition of development, the anthropocentric bias of the statement [sustainability] springs to mind; it is not the preservation of nature's dignity which is on the international agenda, but to extend human-centred utilitarianism to posterity.[13]

Resources – as we like to call matter for which we have a commercial use – are being transformed at a speed far beyond the natural self-renewing rate of the biosphere. Consequently, reserves of useful matter are running low and many will soon have vanished. 'The human race was fortunate enough to inherit a 3.8 billion-year-old reserve of natural capital.'[14] At present rates of consumption, it is predicted as unlikely that there will be much of it left by the end of this century. 'Since the mid 18th century, more of nature has been destroyed than in all prior history.'[15] During the past 50 years alone, the human race has stripped the world of a quarter of its topsoil and a third of its forest cover. 'In total, one third of all the planet's resources have been consumed within the past four decades.'[16]

Design for sustainability?

The designing of new lifestyles running in tighter synchrony with natural systems was first credibly proposed as far back as the 13th century. German theologian Meister Eckhart frequently conceptualized Earth as a fragile and sensitive resource affected by human endeavour; so concern for the natural environment is anything but a contemporary malaise. During the early 1800s, upper-class lovers of the great outdoors were amongst the first to balk at the timber industry's brutal harvesting of ancient woodlands; yet their cries were motivated by aesthetic values rather than a threat to local biodiversity or the loss of natural air filtration.

In late 19th-century Britain, at the dawn of the decadent Arts and Crafts period, early connections between emergent cultures of superfluous materialism and environmental decay were acknowledged. The extravagant modes of consumption spawned by the prolific pace of post-industrial revolution manufacturing were steadily corrupting the biosphere, causing growing concern for the more enlightened industrialists. In time, these sentiments began to percolate into the creative practice of design luminaries such as Charles Eames, Frank Lloyd Wright and Richard Buckminster Fuller. The works of these and a handful of other early revolutionaries, including William Morris and Marcel Breuer, provide living testimony to the design industry's first tentative steps toward a sustainable future.

During the last 40 years, countless strategic approaches to sustainable design from the bizarre to the banal have circulated the more progressive creative ponds. The sheer diversity of strategies within the sustainable designer's toolbox illustrates both the multifaceted nature of the environmental paradigm and the vast range of approaches taken by designers today. Many of these approaches focus purely on specific stages of the product life cycle; these are generically referred to as Design for X (DfX) strategies. DfX strategies, including design for disassembly, design for recycling and design for re-use, are increasingly deployed by the white goods, electronics and automotive sectors where legislative demand for waste minimization is mounting fast.

Other popular strategies include alternative energies, from solar to human power; sourcing local materials and processes; collapsible objects to conserve landfill space; supply chain management; zero emissions; compostable products; and a growing left-field interest in edible packaging, to name but a small handful. Today's sustainable design creative also has access to an extensive palette of low-impact materials from recycled polymers such as polythene and polypropylene, to metals such as steel, aluminium and brass. Other materials include textiles made from sustainably harvested plant fibres, energy-efficient structural cardboard for architectural applications, high-performance biodegradable plastics made from vegetable starch, and a host of other strangely seductive compounds to shape the future. Aided further by a rich resource of seminal texts by such key thinkers as Victor Papanek, Nigel Whiteley, Ed van Hinte, Fritz Schumacher and Ezio Manzini, a new wave of designers with potent environmental agendas is in emergence – designers who realize the potential they possess to slow down environmental decay through elegant, efficient and responsible solutions.

Consumer markets are becoming increasingly aware of the social, environmental and personal implications of their purchasing decisions. Research carried out by *ES Magazine* in 2000 shows that a massive 75 per cent of consumers claim to favour products with tangible environmental advantages over competitive products. 'Three-quarters of the people polled in the UK say that they would make a choice of products on a green or ethical basis, and 28 per cent say that they actually have chosen or boycotted a product or company for ethical reasons over the past 12 months.'[17] This indicates that the future survival of many large brands will become increasingly dependent upon both the delivery and perceptibility of eco-conscious practices and products. *ES Magazine* then goes on to state that 86 per cent of British consumers say that they have a more positive image of a company if they see it doing something to make the world a better place.

Sustainable design is no longer regarded by the wider creative industry as a whimsical mutation of design proper, and environmental factors such as design for disassembly and the specification of low-impact materials are increasingly integrated to conventional design practice without ceremony and to reasonably lucrative ends. In addition, we now know that sustainability is compatible with economic growth, and should begin to push this notion forward with far greater confidence. In 1999 the *Dow Jones Sustainability Group Index* was set up to track shareholder value in companies that integrate both environmental and economic factors. The pilot analysis suggested that 'efforts to promote environmental sustainability do not have to come at the expense of competitiveness'.[18]

Consumption and waste

The rampant consumption and waste of natural resources so prevalent in the developed world is a legacy of modern times, born largely from the inappropriate marriage of excessive material durability with fleeting product-use careers. 'Some products are discarded before they are physically worn out or are technically superseded because their design is out of fashion or inappropriate to changed circumstances.'[19] In other words, the injection-moulded styrene shell that houses the electronic components for a mini disc (MD) player will take about 500 years to degrade fully before slowly returning back to the Earth's energy cycles. Yet, we are all aware that even a four-year use career might be considered a triumph in the case of such a format dependent product. Like its jilted cassette-playing predecessors, the MD player is likely to touch landfill only five or six years after leaving the production line – a short life, indeed, for such a durable object.

Over 90 per cent of the resources taken out of the ground today become waste within only three months: waste consisting of plastics, metals and other synthetic compounds no longer recognizable to the microbial decomposers that degrade substances back to their basic nutritional building blocks. Within this development lies a potential problem: waste.

An apt example of this manner of natural resource transformation is oil. Oil is a substance that will degrade in its original state, but becomes an unstable biohazard once turned into plastic, which has been projected to take as long as 4000 years, in some cases, to degrade fully. Even biodegradable waste such as paper, wood and other vegetable-based compounds escape decomposition as overloaded landfills lack the correct mix of water, oxygen and light for nature's microbial banquet to occur. 'In anthropological studies of the Fresh Kills Landfill Site in New York, hotdogs, corncobs and newspapers that were 25 years' old were still in recognizable form, and the newspapers were readable.'[20] It therefore appears clear that biodegradability – although a theoretically bright idea – rarely functions in the mass quantities that we expect it to.

Although the profitability of consumer durables has been a source of great commercial fascination for decades, commercial:

> ... interest in the life span of consumer durables started in the late 1950s when Vance Packard, in his book *The Waste Makers*, coined the phrase 'planned obsolescence'. There was great interest at that time in the deliberate shortening of life spans by manufacturers. Throughout the 1960s, many people

expressed concern at this trend, but not much happened in response. In 1982 the Organisation for Economic Co-operation and Development (OECD) produced its report *Product Durability and Product Life Extension*; but again little practical action followed.[21]

The prevailing industrial model of the time prescribed the transient and grossly inefficient system of consumption that we fumble through today; consumers of the 1900s were not born wasteful, they were trained to be so by the sales-hungry teachings of a handful of industries bent on market domination. It is tragic to note that the effects of these 20th-century teachings live on today through our wastefully short-term engagements with the made world.

Sustainable design is symptom focused

Despite diversity, in their current guise sustainable design methodologies lack philosophical depth, adopting a symptom-focused approach comparable with that of Western medicine. Many healthcare professionals candidly admit that Western medical practice is frequently more concerned with the suppression of undesirable symptoms than with the actual restoration of health *per se*. If a patient has a headache, for example, a Western doctor will most likely prescribe drugs to mask the pain with little regard to what may be causing the discomfort. Experienced Chinese medical practitioners state that over 50 per cent of headaches are caused by the body's inability to detoxify as a result of mild dehydration, and is thus curable by simply drinking a large glass of water. However, it would be inaccurate to adopt a pro-Oriental stance when it comes to environmental conduct, as the common practice of burying mountains of post-consumer waste out of sight and out of mind is equally prolific in the developed East. For decades, the developed world consumer machine has raged forth practically unchanged, leaving designers to attend the periphery, healing mere symptoms of what is, in essence, a fundamentally flawed system.

Amidst the frantic scramble to comply with growing legislative demands, the root causes of the ecological crisis that we face are frequently overlooked. Meanwhile, consumers continue wastefully on, but do so, now, with recycled materials instead of virgin ones. Although advantageous in a number of scenarios, recycling alone is not a one-stop solution to sustainable production and consumption; it represents only a small part of a far wider picture. Many researchers are beginning to suspect that recycling actually provides an ethical 'get out of jail free card', which liberates consumer conscience and, in so doing, generates even more waste.

> Eco-design limits itself to an environmental technological approach and recycling is sometimes even an excuse for more rapid discarding.[22]

Sustainable design has developed a tendency to focus on the symptoms of the ecological crisis rather than the actual causes. In consequence, deeper strategic possibilities are overlooked, which if developed might build further value into existing creative methodologies. By failing to understand the actual drivers underpinning the human consumption and waste of goods, sustainable design resigns itself to a peripheral activity, rather than the central pioneer of positive social change that it potentially could be.

Tweaking typologies

Through a wide-eyed affection for all things new, mainstream industrial design has become technocentric, incorporating contemporary technologies within archaic product typologies – a skin deep discipline devoid of rich content that packages culture into slick consumable bytes, streamlined with synthetic polymers and metals:

> We do amazing things with technology, and we're filling the world with amazing systems and devices; but we find it hard to explain what this new stuff is for, or what value it adds to our lives. I don't think we can evade these questions any longer... Do all these chips make for better products? Or a better life? Let me tell you a strange thing. Hardly anyone is asking that question. When it comes to innovation, we are looking down the wrong end of the telescope: away from people, toward technology. Industry suffers from a kind of global autism. Autism, as you may know, is a psychological disorder that is characterized by detachment from other human beings.[23]

Like moths around a flame, we are hopelessly seduced by the incandescent glow of all things modern, be it a flatter screen or a smarter plastic, while remaining largely oblivious to the astonishing potential lurking within deeper, poetic, semantic and interactive product developments. Technological innovation is a vital element of the developmental design process yet, in recent years, it has taken centre stage at the expense of other less tangible, though equally potent, creative considerations. In so doing, technocentric design has inadvertently authored a grossly transient culture of wasteful consumerism burdened with the unattainable task of sustaining closeness to the state of the art:

> Because everything moves so fast, and we cannot stop it, we have to create some islands of slowness. Design, in all its history, but especially in more recent years, has been an agent of acceleration. Is it possible to conceive of solutions combining real-time interactions with the possibility of taking time for thinking and contemplation?[24]

Designers are not solely responsible for today's restless culture of continually tweaking product typologies; consumers also possess ardent interest in technological artefacts, not only for their utilitarian capabilities, but also for their rendering of human creativity made perceivable and experienceable. Products provide a tangible means for us to engage with the world on this abstract level, and the motivators underpinning the drive to consume are powerfully influenced by emotional and psychological factors such as these. Since the first person dissected one smooth stone into two sharp-edged cutting tools, we have been mesmerized by objects that signify characteristics of human brilliance, affording elevated social status to individuals in possession of such artefacts.

The myth of individuality

During the latter stages of the 19th century, Swiss linguist Ferdinand de Saussure worked through the concept of the sign, developed from Plato's idea – from *Cratylus* – of the signifier to the signified. He argued that relationships between the signifier and signified are arbitrary and that signs are only meaningful in relation to one another – for example, light and dark, hot and cold, or mutton and lamb. As defined most simply in the *Tao*

Te Ching, 'from dark emerges light, which in its own nature gives birth to darkness once more'.[25]

In 1982, French philosopher Jacques Derrida, in his analysis of *difference*, emphasizes this point once more in propounding the theory that meaning cannot be found within the signifier itself, but that it can only exist in a matrix and, therefore, in relation to other things. Signifiers form meaningful networks to which we have very little conscious access, but which affect our lives completely; they organize our world as we unconsciously organize and manipulate them. With the idea of singularity and separatism in question, Derrida further claims that there can be no absolute identity: 'nothing that is itself by virtue of its being'.[26] Nothing stands outside the system of differences, and we must be co-dependent with the other in order to experience the self. There can, therefore, be no such reality as an individual as separate from society, just as there cannot be a societal mass without the presence of individuals. Society provides a mirror through which each individual person may assess his or her own hierarchical position; such comparisons within one's immediate societal group are a fundamental survival tool.

Today, material possessions are increasingly deployed as signifiers of status, casting us within socially desirable roles and stimulating an edgy culture of habitual comparing that is also prevalent in many other herding species. For example, a gazelle's survival is based almost exclusively upon relative stealth within the herd. Predators inexhaustibly pursue the group in search of stragglers, and so the key to success on the gazelle highway is not about being the fastest but avoiding being the slowest. Capitalist societies aspire to a different brand of success measured predominantly by wealth, and though the props differ radically from that of the societal gazelle, individual pressure to keep up with the group is equally acute.

Jamming creativity

Aesthetic fallout from technocentric design includes the stagnation of product typologies. Although an object's functional array may be incrementally tweaked with finite technological developments, the nature and complexity of the relationships most products hold with users remain unchanged. In their 30-year existence, desktop personal computers (PCs)

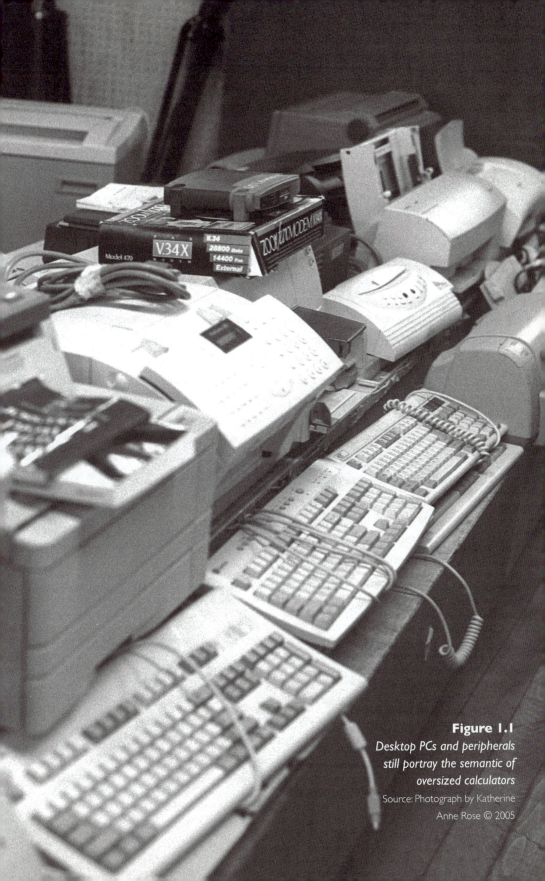

Figure 1.1
*Desktop PCs and peripherals
still portray the semantic of
oversized calculators*
Source: Photograph by Katherine
Anne Rose © 2005

have evolved little despite significant developments in their productive capabilities. Even after the developed world market's quantum shift from office to home use during the late 1990s, computers continue to portray the semantic of oversized calculators. This wrongfully presupposes that all consumer side issues have already been adequately defined, and the needs of the computer user are the same today as they were back in 1970.

In 1998, Apple utilized this barren aesthetic as a backdrop for their first litter of multicoloured 'must haves'. Market share was won and the societal gains afforded by the iMac, and later the iBook, came as timely reappraisal of our relationship with digital technology, challenging convention by introducing alternative and fresh futures. Stagnant portrayals of reality, such as the desktop PC, deliver consumers a stream of serial disappointments by failing to maintain currency with the ever evolving values and needs of the user, streaming material life into one socially approved yet flagrantly outdated version. Interestingly, it often takes the introduction of a radical concept – or simply the introduction of an unfamiliar way to undertake familiar tasks – for users to actually stand back and recognize the sheer banality of the objects with which they have been mindlessly interacting up to that point: like listening to some really dire music, you often are not aware of how terrible it is until it stops. This is why it is so crucial that users are presented with a variety of objects, with each approaching a similar task in a different and wholly unique way – some rational and task focused, others bizarre and richly experiential, and so on. Needless to say, the current model of industrial design does not follow this route; perhaps due to the pressures of commercialism, the industry collectively gangs together and hits users with a somewhat monotonous stream of very similar objects.

Although most design concepts exit the cranium as fairly eccentric manifestations, like rocks on a riverbed they are inadvertently streamlined over time until more socially comprehensive scenarios are realized. Pared down to their simplest form, object types from toasters to televisions are recognizable at a glance due to a handful of prominent visual signatures, providing semiotic signage to clearly inform consumers of an object's assigned role and purpose. Through aesthetic discourse between creative designers and researchers, consumers and marketing specialists, consensus

Figure 1.2
The notion of choice is somewhat limited when interacting with the offerings of contemporary material culture
Source: Photograph by Katherine Anne Rose © 2005

is reached regarding the way things should look; a mug is a ceramic cylinder with one semicircular handle, and laptops are like plastic books with keys and a screen. In a world of constantly evolving social values, static design languages such as these are obscure, to say the least. Problems increasingly occur when contemporary design scenarios cannot be easily pigeonholed into any one predefined type, jamming both creative freedom and real opportunities for change.

How to guarantee disappointment

Rigid product typologies set the aesthetic parameters within which conventional design may freely function; any ventures beyond these guidelines plunge us into fuzzy, uncomfortable territory where genres blur and meanings cross-pollinate. In some instances, universally understood design languages are necessary, particularly in the case of safety equipment or highway signage where information must be instantly cognized without error. However, in its current state, industrial design prefers to safely dwell within the superficial security of these parameters, channelling its innovative energy solely toward the incorporation of new technologies into predefined product types. 'Interacting with this technocratic and de-personalized environment fuels a reactionary mind set that hankers after meaningful content, mystery and emotion.'[27] Both the range and intensity of emotional experiences delivered by products born of this mindset are incredibly limited and offer very little to the consumer. 'Yet, even though industrial design plays a part in the design of extreme pain (e.g. weapons) and pleasure (e.g. sex aids), the range of emotions offered through most electronic products is pathetically narrow.'[28] Industrial design has become a subordinate packager of contemporary technologies, housing intangible hardware within intelligible synthetic membranes whose purpose is to enable consumers to easily interact without altercation or thought.

Cosmetic approaches to design engender wasteful cycles of desire and frustration within consumers by delivering only short-lived glimpses of progress. Placing technological currency as the sole product value-indicator ensures loss of meaning the moment a newer model hits the shelves. In a marketplace of relentless product obsolescence, the notion of consumer satisfaction will continue to remain a tantalizing utopia until product values diversify to incorporate factors beyond technical modernity – enabling consumers to transcend the temporal urgency of technocentric design and engage with their possessions over greater periods of time, and on a diversity of emotional and experiential levels.

The volume of waste produced by this cyclic pattern of short-term desire and disappointment is a major problem, not just in terms of space and where to put it, but, perhaps more notably, for its toxic corruption of the biosphere. The majority of today's post-consumer waste is currently disposed of via landfill sites, which leak heavy metals and other toxic contaminants over time, such as arsenic, cadmium, copper, lead, manganese and zinc. These toxic elements find their way into soil and groundwater, threatening local biodiversity. Landfills are also known to produce large volumes of methane, a principal greenhouse gas contributing to global warming. A smaller percentage of waste is burned using vast incinerators that produce ash laden with toxic elements such as cadmium, lead, mercury, chromium, tin and zinc, while also releasing acidic gases such as sulphur dioxide and nitrous oxides into the atmosphere. Even the much acclaimed recycling of waste consumes large quantities of energy, while the chemicals involved during treatment and sorting often find their way back into the ecosystem, causing further damage.

Chasing unattainable destinies

As the human population continues to multiply and the quantities of natural resources available per person plummet, a dramatic reappraisal of our wasteful consumption and production is urgently required. Technocentric design is certainly here to stay and will always be one of a number of creative genres to circulate the made world; yet its popularity will surely fade as consumers tire of chasing unattainable destinies. This will give way to new specialist genres of design and consumption fuelled by darker, and more meaningful, user experiences. New product genres will emerge, offering alternatives to the wasteful mode of technocentric design and consumption, expanding our experience of daily life, rather than stifling it through endless cycles of desire and disappointment.

Emotionally durable design

Far beyond the ephemeral world of technocentric design lurks a rich
and interactive domain founded on a profound human need: the need
for empathy. A sustainable realm where natural resources need not be
ravaged to satisfy every fleeting human whim and the very notion of waste
is obsolete. In this utopian futurescape, users and products flourish within
long-lasting empathic partnerships, blissfully oblivious to the relentless
taunts of the capitalist machine. Radical new commercial environments are
pioneered in which objects provide conversation pieces that link consumers
with manufacturers, facilitating upgrade, servicing and repair.

Non-technocentric object genres must emerge motivated by
deeper factors than simply the habitual acquisition of newer, shinier things
delivering profound and sophisticated user experiences that penetrate
the psyche over time. This designable future, so devoid of obsolescence,
waste and serial dissatisfactions, is filled only with attachment, evolution and
mutual growth. A revolutionary consumer reality is born, catalysed by new
and provocative genres of emotionally durable objects and experiences that
are designed for empathy.

Meaningful embraces with objects

The 20th century witnessed a steady societal migration away from deep
communal values toward a fast-food culture of nomadic individualism
and excessive materialism. During recent years, there has been a move
away from interpersonal relationships toward a newer and faster mode
of relations; a significant shift occurred from inter-human relationships
toward a contemporary mode of individuality fragmented over countless
relationships with designed experiences. This epoch-making societal
transition has cast us within an abstract version of reality in which empathy
and meaning are sought from toasters, mobile phones and other fabricated
experiences. Today, empathy is consumed not so much from each other, but
through fleeting embraces with designed objects:

> The shift, away from immateriality and anonymous experience towards
> reflexive encounters, is seemingly only the crest of a larger cultural wave which

is rapidly imparting greater understanding into the way we perceive, condition and create the world in which we live.[29]

This has fostered a mind shift within the development of both object- and human-centred relationships, driving a steady societal shift away from deep communal mutuality toward a fast culture of individualism and superfluous materialism. As experience-hungry users, we are constantly topping up these relationships with newer, and ever more diverse, things.

This behavioural pattern begins to explain the current exudation of waste. Furthermore, in a world of unceasing technological miniaturization, demands will emerge for objects with potent sensory and emotional resonance. We are already beginning to see early signs of a rising consumer desire for products embodying traits of consciousness, eccentricity and an increased responsiveness to emotional input. Autonomous characteristics such as these will be increasingly required to compensate the lack of physical presence resulting from product miniaturization.

Each of us shares, to varying degrees, the need for a material world: a world of tangible things to enhance the experiential quality of daily life, such as a faster car, a larger TV or a softer sofa. However, along with these enhancements to the experiential fabric of daily life, these physical objects serve a deeper and altogether more profound purpose that is frequently overlooked; consumable objects and experiences provide a means for us of engaging with the world on both rational and emotional levels. In the instance of a new laptop, for example, what we see and what we experience are two remarkably different things. In one sense, we see a slick plastic chassis and assume that inside is a battery, a disk drive of some sort and extensive complex circuitry that we will most likely never actually see, but can confidently assume it is in there somewhere. What we experience, on the other hand, might include intense sensations of freedom, independence, control, individuality, efficiency, precision, organization and status. These experiences portray consumable utopias perceived from within the products semantic – utopias that are boldly promised, yet seldom realized, depositing unrealistic expectations within consumers.

Waste is symptomatic of failed relationships

Developed world consumer desires relentlessly grow and flex, while material possessions remain hopelessly frozen in time. This incapacity for mutual evolution renders most products incapable of sustaining a durable relationship with users. The mountain of waste this single inconsistency generates is apocalyptic, coming at increasing cost to legislation-swamped manufacturers and the natural world. Landfills around the globe swell with fully functional appliances – freezers that still freeze and toasters that still toast – their only crime being a failure to sustain empathy with their users. Research has shown that, during recent years, '25 per cent of vacuum cleaners, 60 per cent of stereos and even 90 per cent of computers still function when people get rid of them.'[30]

For centuries, the art world has been implicitly aware of the need for mutual evolution between the consumer and the consumed. Artistic expressions from traditional oil paintings to *avant-garde* installations are conceived as contemplative works, rarely surrendering all their meaning at a single glance. This is enabled by the presence not simply of meaning, but of layers of meaning that continually tantalize the onlooker to provide a lifetime of incremental revelations. In 1912, German psychologist Theodor Lipps propounded the theory that the appreciation of a work of art depended upon the capacity of the spectator to project his personality into the object of contemplation. Lipps claimed that 'one had to feel oneself into it'.[31] He named this cybernetic process *Einfuhlung*, which translates as 'empathy'. In their current guise, consumer products lack the sophistication and layered complexity for this degree of long-term empathy to incubate. Most consumer products relinquish their tenuous meaning to a single fleeting glance, while rarely delivering any of the life-altering rewards they so confidently promise. In this respect, waste is nothing more than symptomatic of a failed user/object relationship, where insufficient empathy led to the perfunctory dumping of one by the other.

In terms of sustainability, it appears rational to assume that extending product lifetimes will have a wholly positive outcome; yet, as with most things, all is not as simple as it may first appear. In the instance of energy consumption and the energy efficiency of consumer appliances, for example, the product life debate widens further still. Objects such as walking sticks and door handles that consume little or no energy through use can, and should, theoretically go on living forever, whereas products such as vacuum cleaners and ovens that require greater amounts of energy to function may require a closer look. Take the humble refrigerator, for example; being the largest consumers of electricity in the average household, refrigerators receive a large share of annual research and development budgets. Consequently, incremental improvements in energy efficiency are in abundance. It therefore follows that to run an energy-hungry yet cherished 1950s classic may not be the smart move in terms of energy consumption, and it would be worthy of speculation whether the energy consumed by such a product in a two- to three-year period might actually be more than that required to process the materials and manufacture an entirely new and more efficient one. Despite this analysis, research into the elongation of product life must still surge forth. Perhaps the inefficient motor in the 1950s fridge simply needs replacing with a newer and more efficient one which, like a heart transplant, might afford the old fridge a new lease of life.

Anthropocentrism

Since the closing stages of the 20th century, sustainability – as a term of reference – has found its way to the very forefront of modern culture to the point that the word has now become a vital addition to our daily vocabulary. Despite the growing popularity of this term, it must be questioned as to whether we actually understand it, what it signifies; and what it proposes we do as a solution-focused society. Though well intentioned, sustainability in itself could be described as a deeply anthropocentric premise:

> … people like to preserve these things not because they perform some important function in their own right, but, rather, because they wish to ensure that people will be serviced in the future in exactly the same way they are currently.[32]

Even the word 'ecology' is taken from the Greek *oikos*, meaning house or household: the immediate human environment.

Anthropocentric thinking is commonplace in the growing knowledge field of environmental sustainability, and frequently serves to place our species at the forefront of all significant disasters on the Earth. We see ourselves as being so powerful and magnificent that our abilities have outgrown this fragile planet's ability to support us. This self-elevating arrogance is surprisingly evident within a large percentage of ecological thinking, and we must move beyond this counterproductive rendering of self if we are to benefit the wider environmental cause. The way in which we perceive our own supremacy as a species can be further demonstrated via the common assumption that if aliens came to this planet, they would, of course, want to make contact with and study humans. Would they really? They may actually be far more interested in sand, turnips or grasshopper wings.

Take global warming, for example; it is beyond dispute that the greenhouse effect is, indeed, a real and potentially deadly threat and that global warming is going to cause immeasurable problems. But let us not get ahead of ourselves. The Earth's climate has always been unstable, and sea levels have been rising and falling since the very dawn of time. It could be said that like everything else on this unstable planet, transience is one of our climate's key characteristics, and it is important that we remain mindful of this. After all, the ice age was surely not triggered by our lack of polluting at that time or, perhaps, insufficient burning of fossil fuels. A continually fluctuating global climate is a natural condition of the planet, and though we obviously contribute in a major way to global warming, the enormity of climate change suggests that greater forces are at work, and that it may not be entirely down to us.

Many well-respected practitioners within the sustainable arena believe that 'the definition of sustainability is neither vague nor abstract; it is very specific and is tied to measurable criteria describing how resources are used and distributed.'[33] In addition to this, many ardent supporters of sustainability will refuse to even consider the possibility of objection, believing that a unanimous consensus must be reached in which everyone agrees with the moral principles laid down by the ethical ideologies of sustainability. Nevertheless:

> Sustainable planning policy in Europe rests on an extreme degree of consensus, that sustainability is right. There is no ethical basis for this. An extreme consensus can in itself be unethical. In its most abstract form, sustainability has no inherent value. The standard argument for recent sustainability policy – transgenerational responsibility – has no inherent ethical status either.
>
> In practice, sustainable planning continues standard practice, and this offers the best explanation for its success. Sustainability is an ideology used to justify existing policy (and social order).[34]

Despite the positive motives underlying most people's engagement with sustainability, it must be noted that the very term sustainable is actually quite unhelpful. It defines the concept in such broad terms that it may be applied to almost any endeavour that loosely shares its vague ideologies; what are we sustaining, and for how long should we sustain it? The term has become so overused that most of its desired impact has been lost, and like most popular slogans it is beginning to wear rather thin:

> The word sustainable has been slapped onto everything from sustainable forestry to sustainable agriculture, sustainable economic growth, sustainable development, sustainable communities and sustainable energy production. The widespread use of the term indicates that many people conclude that the dominant industrial models of production are unsustainable.[35]

Despite this analysis, many still argue in favour of the term, stating that 'we don't need a theory of sustainability. We already know what it is and even if we don't know, it is a motivating slogan for social change.'[36] Participating in the sustainability debate through such means as buying local, consuming alternative energy or, perhaps, being proactive in a neighbourhood recycling initiative provides many with an enormous sense of well-being. And there is nothing wrong with that. The same may be said of other ethically aware practices, such as buying organic. Research from the UK supermarket Sainsbury's revealed that a large number of their customers chose organic produce because it gave them a sense of well-being, rather than any particular concern for the environment or, perhaps, their health. Although those of us who ride our bikes to the bottle banks while nibbling on an organic carrot might deny that we get a huge kick out of doing our bit for the environment, it is essentially of little consequence. The important thing is that we are engaging in acts of positive social and ecological change, whatever our motives might be.

About-face

Einstein once stated that a problem could not be solved from within the mindset that created it. Indeed, fresh thinking is imperative if we are to successfully transcend current working methods and stride forth into unprecedented commercial territories. *Emotionally Durable Design* reframes the environmental paradigm, increasing resource productivity and reducing waste by elongating the lifespan of products.

This book proposes a radical design about-face in order to reduce the impact of modern consumption without compromising commercial or creative edge – empowering alternative modes of consumption through provocative genres of objects that expand our experience of daily life, rather than closing it down through endless cycles of desire and disappointment. This book does not propose a sweeping overhaul of the entire designed world. Instead, it espouses the emergence of a specialist design genre that caters for deeper, more profound and poetic human needs, taking users beyond the ephemeral world of technocentric design toward a rich, interactive domain of emotionally durable objects and experiences. 'It is time for a new generation of products that can age slowly and in a dignified way … [to] become our partners in life and support our memories.'[37]

Emotionally Durable Design is an exploration into product lifetimes; belonging to the growing knowledge field of sustainable design, this book essentially embarks upon an investigation into why users dispose of products that still work, while providing designers from a range of creative disciplines with a toolbox of inspiring strategies to extend product life, interlaced with insightful critiques of the motivational drivers that underpin the human consumption and waste of goods. *Emotionally Durable Design* is not a moralizing tale, nor does it claim to present any singular universal truth. Rather, like a much needed food parcel strategically dropped into a defined region of growing concern, this research delivers timely reappraisal of both economic and environmental sustainability in a destructive age of transient design, consumption and grossly misplaced sustainable agendas.

Chapter summary

Environmental concern is nothing new; recorded awareness of human impact on the biosphere dates as far back as the 13th century.
. . . .

Connections between emergent cultures of superfluous materialism and environmental decay were acknowledged in late 19th-century Britain at the dawn of the decadent Arts and Crafts period.
. . . .

Population growth alone is not a problem for planet Earth; the growth of a species whose presence has negative impacts on all other life must be seen as a potential ecological crisis.
. . . .

The rampant consumption and waste of natural resources so prevalent in the developed world is a legacy of modern times, born largely from the inappropriate marriage of excessive material durability with fleeting product-use careers.
. . . .

In their current guise, sustainable design methodologies lack philosophical depth, adopting a symptom-focused approach comparable to that of Western medicine.
. . . .

Despite the efforts of sustainable design, today's consumers continue wastefully on, but now with recycled materials instead of virgin ones.
. . . .

Many researchers are beginning to suspect that recycling actually provides an ethical 'get out of jail free' card, liberating consumer conscience and generating even more waste.
. . . .

The future survival of many large brands will become increasingly dependent upon both the delivery and perceptibility of eco-conscious practices and products.
. . . .

Mainstream industrial design has become technocentric, incorporating contemporary technologies within archaic product typologies.
. . . .

During recent years, technological innovation has taken centre stage at the expense of other less tangible, though equally potent, creative considerations.

· ·

Material possessions are deployed as signifiers of status, casting us within socially desirable roles, stimulating edgy cultures of habitual comparing.

· ·

Both the range and intensity of emotional experiences delivered by products born of a technocentric mindset are incredibly limited and offer very little to users.

· ·

Placing technological contemporaneousness as the sole product value-indicator ensures loss of meaning the moment a newer model hits the shelves.

· ·

Technocentric design will fade as consumers tire of chasing unattainable utopias, giving way to new specialist genres of design and consumption fuelled by more profound and poetic user experiences that penetrate the psyche over time.

· ·

The 20th century witnessed a steady societal migration away from deep communal values toward a fast-food culture of nomadic individualism and excessive materialism; today, empathy is consumed not so much from each other, but through fleeting embraces with objects.

· ·

Developed world consumer desires relentlessly grow and flex, while material possessions remain hopelessly frozen in time. The mountain of waste this single inconsistency generates is apocalyptic, coming at increasing cost to legislation-swamped manufacturers and the natural world.

· ·

Landfills around the word swell with fully functional appliances — freezers that still freeze and toasters that still toast — their only crime being a failure to sustain empathy with their users.

· ·

Emotionally Durable Design will transport users beyond the ephemeral world of technocentric design toward a rich, interactive domain of emotionally durable objects and experiences.

· ·

A toolbox of ideas

Environment as user: when attempting to engage with sustainability, think of the environment as just another end user – a user with specific needs, demands and limitations. It follows that good design, therefore, will aim to accommodate the requirements of all potential users: corporate, consumer and environment.

. . . .

Material life: when planning product lifespan, consider the lifespan of the materials from which the product is made. For example, renewable materials from the biosphere, including compostable plant-based composites and biopolymers, all offer designers a short-lived and low-impact alternative to the recyclable, but all too durable, plastics, elastomers and resins that are so widely used today; immune to the glare of biological decay, these materials grossly outlive our desire for them.

. . . .

Causes not symptoms: adopt the philosophy of ancient Chinese medicine; focus on the causes of our environmental destruction, not just on how to clean up or minimize the obvious after-effects. Rather than solely addressing waste, target and design for the motivations underpinning it; this is where the fundamental changes lurk.

. . . .

Poetic potential: think beyond technological modernity by exploring the potential for other, more poetic, experiential and interactive forms of product evolution and innovation – embedding less transient, enduring values within products that may be sustained through the slow passing of time.

chapter
two

consumer
motivation

Consumption is natural

Ask a developed world human to stop consuming and you might as well
ask a vampire not to suck blood. Although the urge can be temporarily
suppressed to varying degrees of success, over-compensatory surges
inevitably follow, providing an aftermath of even greater intensity;
consumption is not just a way of life, it is life. It provides an invaluable
vehicle for processing and interacting with an evolving world, facilitating
both learning and social interaction through the continual intake of new,
fresh experiences. As natural as drawing breath, the urge to consume
is merely symptomatic of a stimulus-hungry species dwelling in a
homogenized and over-streamlined world where the prevailing mode of
existence comes with the majority of problems already solved. This reduces
the once life-threatening natural world down to a whimsical pastime now
experienced in 30-minute bytes through televised portals such as The
Discovery Channel, Wildlife on One and Animal Planet.

Indeed, as our tools have improved, we suddenly find ourselves
with large amounts of spare time that need filling; complex and often highly
specialized tasks that once may have taken hours to accomplish can now

be solved by all in a matter of seconds. Crippled by its own brilliance, the under-stimulated human brain must now search elsewhere for stimulation of a more synthetic, designed nature. The modern consumer is born and shall, henceforth, mine the glossy veneers of material culture in the hopeless pursuit of qualitative stimulation.

The material you possess is the destiny you chase

Like an itch that can never be scratched, the covetous search for the ultimate expression of self as mediated through manufactured objects appears to be endless:

> The people I know who used to sit in the bathroom with pornography, now they sit in the bathroom with their IKEA furniture catalogue… You buy furniture. You tell yourself, this is the last sofa I will ever need in my life. Buy the sofa, then for a couple of years you're satisfied that no matter what goes wrong, at least you've got your sofa issue handled. Then the right set of dishes. Then the perfect bed. The drapes. The rug.[1]

This customary behavioural process of continual aspiration and self-improvement is relentless and, as most of us have experienced first hand, seldom arrives at the utopian destination that it so desperately strives to reach.

Material consumption is driven by complex motivations and is about far more than just the acquisition of newer, shinier things. It is an endless personal journey toward the ideal or desired self that by its very nature becomes a process of incremental destruction; this take-up and subsequent displacement of matter enables the consumer to perceive their individual evolution and development as it occurs ontologically:

> Modern consumption conveys an approach of selecting unique products that meet specific values and lifestyles, and is manifested in the desire to buy products that satisfy perceived lifestyle preferences … it represents a consumption pattern that is designed to pursue a unique way of life and which differs from that of other people.[2]

Figure 2.1

Consumption is about far more than just
the acquisition of new and shiny things

Source: Photograph by Katherine
Anne Rose © 2005

Designed objects and experiences provide a tangible means for us to engage with the world on this existential level, and the potency of objects in symbolically designating our particular being cannot be overstated.

Despite the environmentally conscious whitewash of negativity that comes hand in hand with the process of consumption, it must not simply be cast off as a fruitless sequence of material destruction; far greater things are taking place which, if examined, may provide further insight into the gross inefficiencies of contemporary material culture. Contrary to popular wisdom, the process of consumption occurs constantly – even now through the intake of the meanings that these printed words signify; therefore, metaphysically, we are continually engaged within this process. While doctors may claim we are consumers of oxygen, water and sunlight from the moment of conception, a philosopher might speak of existence as the opportunity to consume knowledge and experience. The majority view, however, is still grossly misguided in assuming that consumption only occurs when credit cards are taken out. It has become commonplace throughout all media, from ecological journals and corporate websites to popular television and the tabloid press, to be cautioned on the rampant consumption of goods and the over-consumption of natural resources. Today, the word consumption comes overloaded with negativity, which renders it a blurred and deeply distorted phenomenon, frequently obstructing the lucid comprehension of what is actually a fundamental human behaviour.

The dark side

In ecological circles consumption is spoken of with a practically universal disdain, and not without just cause. Within the last 50 years alone, the world has lost over a quarter of its ancient rain forests, posing a large threat not only to biodiversity but also to the planet's air quality. In addition, both carbon dioxide (CO_2) emissions and the consumption of fossil fuels themselves have increased almost 400 per cent within the same period, catalysing further irreversible devastation to the biosphere. 'US consumers and industry dispose of enough aluminium to rebuild the commercial air fleet every three months [and] enough iron and steel to continuously supply all automakers.'[3] Global climate is already showing signs of mutation, with current projections indicating an average global temperature increase of up 6° Celsius (C) over the next few hundred years. 'For the first time in the history of the world, every human being is now subjected to contact with dangerous chemicals, from the moment of conception until death.'[4] Add to this the mounting problems of waste, acidification of soil and groundwater, deforestation, air pollution, diminishing natural resources, ozone depletion and global warming, then the picture does start to appear somewhat bleak, no matter what your ethical stance may be.

Statistics impose a paralysing vastness

Macpherson states that 'it is certainly a shallow philosophy that would make human welfare synonymous with the indiscriminate production and consumption of material goods'.[5] However, launching into a diatribe of doom and gloom statistics merely labours the already comprehensive axiom: production and consumption in their current guises are both inequitable, and without future. A well-intentioned snowstorm of environmental data may attempt to argue the case for immediate action; yet, in reality, we – as a consumer society – are already aware that our lavish existence is ravaging the Earth. If anything, environmental statistics of this nature actually hinder progress as they adorn the ecological crisis with a paralysing vastness that simply intimidates us as individuals. Such apocalyptic data are counterproductive in most scenarios, and are often the precursor to the murmuring of 'what difference can I possibly make?' The streams of environmental doom and gloom that have been emerging over the past decade contribute enormously to the current problem, where most consumers feel disengaged, lacking in motivation and emotionally numbed by the sheer vastness of our looming ecological crisis.

In reaction to this, in 1990 Greenpeace artfully personified the *Exxon Valdez* disaster by claiming that 'it wasn't the *Exxon Valdez* captain's driving that caused the Alaskan oil spill. It was yours.'[6] In doing so each individual consumer was able to perceive their own personal contribution to what was a vast global crisis, demonstrating that small perceptual shifts will reframe situations in powerfully beneficial ways. Passive consumer attitudes to the ecological crisis we face are enforced further by the misguided preconception that comfort must be sacrificed in order to make positive change, and 'the changes in living that would be required are so drastic that people prefer the future catastrophe to the sacrifice they would have to make now'.[7] Warped notions of ascetic lifestyles abounding with non-enjoyment invade the consumer psyche, rendering the prospect of a greener existence an undesirable alternative; thus, the inefficient consumer machine continues to thrust wastefully forth. Feel-good after measures such as recycling bear grave similarity to 'someone who quits smoking on his deathbed',[8] and in some instances possess an equally negligible efficacy. The emergent culture of ecological procrastination that we see today could also be likened to the common experience of delaying a visit to the dentist. Though perfectly aware that each day brings further discomfort, the decaying tooth goes unattended, ensuring that the inevitable operation will be far more dreadful when it does eventually arrive.

The tuberculosis analogy

The parasitic mode of resource destruction so prevalent within the human species could be likened in structure to that of *Mycobacterium tuberculosis*, the bacillus causing *tuberculosis* (TB). *Mycobacterium tuberculosis* is an opportunist life form with a prolific growth rate. However, like the human species, TB's continually growing populace ensures that its consumption process gathers momentum by the hour. If left untreated, this hostile epidemic will wipe out all absorbable resources until there are simply no more hosts for the virus to migrate to. In other words, TB consumes itself to death. Like TB, we, too, are a race of perpetually dissatisfied consumers 'who never know the worth of water till the well is dry'.[9] Meanwhile the planet's natural reserves deteriorate by the hour, drawing the prospect of a barren, spent world ever nearer.

In the 1999 science fiction epic *The Matrix* — written and directed by Larry and Andy Wachowski — the analogy is taken a step further. A ruthless yet philosophical simulation known as Agent Smith (played by Hugo Weaving) reveals:

I'd like to share a revelation I had during my time here. It came to me when I tried to classify your species. I realized that you're not actually mammals. Every mammal on this planet instinctively develops a natural equilibrium with the surrounding environment; but you humans do not. You move to an area and you multiply until every natural resource is consumed. The only way you can survive is to spread to another area. There is another organism on this planet that follows the same pattern. Do you know what it is? A virus. Human beings are a disease, a cancer of this planet. You are a plague, and we are the cure.[10]

Conceptualizing the act

The devastating environmental impacts of material consumption – such as the diminishing natural resources, air and water pollution, waste and global warming – could be seen as legacies of modern times, catalysed quite simply by the enhanced production capabilities of the 20th century.

A growing awareness of this has led the more enlightened of industrialists to initiate exploration into the possibilities of what they refer to as *sustainable consumption*. At first glance, the term sustainable consumption may appear profoundly oxymoronic: the coupling of two seemingly opposed words. However, on closer inspection it becomes apparent that the actual concept of sustainable consumption is quite possible, though it appears that the meaning of the word *consumption* needs clarifying before any real progress can be made here.

Though the verb *consume* can be traced back to the 14th century, *consumer* emerged much later in 1746, followed later still by *consumerism* in 1944. The verb **consume** derives from the Latin word *consumere*, meaning to use up, eat or waste. An etymological deconstruction thus follows:

> Consume – c1380, from *L. consumere*, 'to use up, eat, waste', from *com*- intensive prefix + *sumere* 'to take', from *sub*- 'under' + *emere* 'to buy, take'. Economic sense of consumer (opposite of producer) first recorded 1746. Consumerism is from 1944 in the sense of 'protection of the consumer's interest'; modern sense of 'consumption as an economic policy' is from 1960.[11]

In the instance of consuming food, it is easy to conceptualize the exchange of both physical and metaphysical property between subject and object. Take an apple, for example: the apple signifies nourishment, vitamins, minerals and an afterglow of vitality to be experienced post-consumption, yet anticipated pre-consumption. To the hungry it represents the potential satisfaction of needs and desires. In the manufactured world the anticipatory exchange of meanings and rewards is similar to that of the apple. The image of a laptop in *T3 Magazine* will speak to the potential consumer of its own intelligence, speed, wit, style and overall ability to project the future user into a contemporary and nomadic world. These perceivable meanings must not be underestimated, as they are feverishly potent to the onlooker. The desire-driven act of consuming the laptop becomes a simple process of embodiment through association and knowledge. Like the apple, nourishment resulting from this type of consumption has a limited lifespan and is largely metaphysical. In the case of manufactured products, the term *consume* can be misleading. Landfills around the globe are swollen full of dishwashers, televisions, hairdryers, computers, mobile phones, answer machines, bicycles, food processors and much more, most of which have spent a year or so of conscience time in the garage prior to being dumped. Many of these products – in a utilitarian sense – still function perfectly and most definitely have not been consumed or used up at all. So what have these apparently indispensable life-changing products ceased to do in order to be granted a 4000-year death sentence of slow biodegradation?

When aren't we consuming?

The motivational drivers underpinning the act of consumption represent a way of being, of interacting with the world. Consumption is far from straightforward and, if anything, the question should be 'when aren't we consuming?' Whether the stimulus is speed, brands, individuality, or anything else for that matter, we are endlessly internalizing external stimuli and will always be engaged within this process. We are consumers of meaning and not matter; it could be argued that material objects simply provide a tangible means through which these connotations may be signified to the user. We transfer resources into products that – in a sense – provide us with existential mirrors, allowing us to view and experience our dreams and desires in real time. These reflections help us to construct an identity that we feel is individual, while also being indicative of our individual aspirations and dreams. In this respect, objects are meaningful in that they illustrate – both to society and the self – our personal life journeys. The process of consumption also appears to possess a quality of avoidance: by continually busying ourselves within a world of goods and services, we cunningly side step sensations of emptiness through sheer distraction – consumption gives us a sense of purpose.

Material consumption operates on a variety of experiential layers, from the rational and the tangible to the profound and the numinous. Consumers mine these layers, unearthing meaningful content as they steadily excavate deeper into the semiotic core of an object. If any one of these layers should fail to stimulate, the relationship between user and object immediately falls under threat. In marketing circles this is referred to as extinction or, more descriptively, as the disappearance of a response due to lack of reinforcement. This is a hazardous stage in the subject–object relationship: hitting rock bottom is frequently the precursor to product replacement. At present, most objects are designed without this understanding, leading to a wasteful culture built on the fragile foundation of anonymous interactions with fairly meaningless objects. In contrast, it may be said that consumers will continue to mine the experiential layers of an object just as long as there are further layers to be mined. It is therefore imperative that designers endeavour to weave greater degrees of intricacy amongst the layers of products to ensure the sustainability of their meaning.

Need

Gandhi once said that 'Earth provides enough to satisfy every man's need, but not every man's greed'.[12] Yet, human need is also insatiable and may quite possibly be situated beyond the reach of complete and total satisfaction. This is because new needs emerge the moment old needs are met, thus nurturing the infinite sequence of desire and destruction so characteristic of the modern world. This continual raising of the bar has brought our society to where it is today both in terms of social and technological evolution. In contrast, our eternal dissatisfaction has also nurtured a grossly transient consumer culture responsible for the crafting of ecological devastation on a global scale. Though well intentioned, attempts to suppress the human need to consume are somewhat futile; swimming against the stream in this way is generally counterproductive. Deeper approaches that are similar in philosophy to the Japanese art of *Aikido*, which aims to both understand and embrace the ensuing problem, may be far more productive. In *Aikido* — meaning *way of integrating the spirit* — an opponent's strength is first understood and then artfully manipulated to gain their control. By understanding more about the very nature of human need, we can begin to manipulate and gain control over it. Only then can we set out to create design solutions to better meet today's ever intensifying levels of consumption.

Need could be described as the very core from which the majority of human motivations are born; continually at work, needs exist as potent psychological features that chastise us into action the moment a lack is experienced. Sociologist Robert Bocock defines the very ideology of consumerism as a vital socio-cultural process, emerging primarily from a sense of lack. 'Consumption is founded on a lack — a desire always for something not there. Modern/post-modern consumers, therefore, will never be satisfied. The more they consume, the more they will desire to consume.'[13] Bocock claims that consumer motivation — or the awakening of human need — is catalysed by a sense of imbalance or lack that steadily cultivates a restless state of being. This restlessness is interpreted by consumers as discontentment, and frequently motivates goal-oriented behaviours such as shopping, discarding or other modifications to the material fabric of one's life. Needs are therefore motivated when a real-time imbalance is experienced between an actual and a desired mode of existence.

Material artefacts are indicative of an individual's aspirations, and serve to outline their desired life direction:

At the most superficial level, an object can be seen by the user to resonate with and be symbolic of the self. Thus, perceiving oneself as rich and powerful might lead to conspicuous consumption, such as owning a luxurious car or wearing designer apparel. At a more profound psychodynamic level, having and utilizing an object can compensate for an unconsciously felt inadequacy.[14]

The advertising industry has been capitalizing on this phenomenon for the last few decades, ensuring that we, as consumers, are exposed to a continual stream of more desirable futures to ensure that a sense of lack is never far away. 'Advertising has us chasing cars and clothes, working jobs we hate so we can buy shit we don't need.'[15] In so doing, consumerism is sustained through the antagonistic nurture of social dissatisfaction that has become so commonplace in modern times that it continues unattended and largely unnoticed. New Zealand's Buy Nothing Day Organization reinforces the notion that a primary endeavour of advertising has been the nurturing of dissatisfaction within consumers; the organization 'believe that advertising abets over-consumption by causing people to feel unfulfilled with what they have, and playing with many personal insecurities, manipulating people into buying more'.[16]

Since the dawn of official consumerism during the 1940s, countless theories have been pioneered that attempt to generate coherent understanding of human need. Many of these attend to the socio-psychological dimensions of the consumer psyche, such as personality differences, status and desire. Other approaches address more peripheral issues such as spending, saving habits and general product preferences. 'As a consequence, only a few consumer researchers have even discussed, much less studied, meaning.'[17] It therefore appears that in research terms, object meaning is a relatively untouched issue and, as a result, exposes a gaping hole in the knowledge field of consumer psychology.

Meaning

The notion of meaning is perhaps the most complex of all: it is influenced by the consumer's previous experiences, while also being highly context specific. For example, the meaning of a rat in a pet shop differs greatly to that of the same rat in a restaurant kitchen. In this respect it is easy to envisage how product meaning can be loosely directed by designers but never fully controlled:

Object meaning incorporates three essential characteristics:
1.   polysemy;
2.   contextual sensitivity; and
3.   consensus.

Polysemy refers to the fact that a given object can mean many things – baking soda, for example, can be a refrigerator deodorizer, a dentifrice or an antacid. Contextual sensitivity suggests that the meaning of a turkey on a Thanksgiving

Day dinner table probably differs from that of a turkey placed on a dinner table during mid May. And consensus refers to the fact that, even though each person holds idiosyncratic information about an object, some minimal amount of object information (meaning) must be shared by people in order for them to communicate about the object.[18]

When discussing the correlation between meaning and function in *Mythologies*, French social and literary critic Roland Barthes stated that the two cannot be separated, and that function is just another meaning. This notion is particularly pertinent in the case of fashion where function is rarely the key designed value. In the case of fashion – particularly high fashion – function serves as a placebo value, a myth that justifies the existence of what is oftentimes a superfluous object. Such mythologies are prolific within today's streamlined world of comfort, where physical needs come in second place to the more resonant pangs of emotional malnourishment.

Having and being

In his seminal book *To Have or To Be*, German social psychologist Erich Fromm pares human motivation down into two basic strands, 'having' and 'being'. According to Fromm 'having' provides an archaic means of possession by enabling the consumer to 'incorporate'[19] the meanings that are signified to them by a given object. In this way consumers are magnetically drawn to objects in possession of that which they subconsciously yearn to become:

> We find the same connection between incorporation and possession in many forms of cannibalism. For example, by eating another human being, I acquire that person's power (thus, cannibalism can be the magic equivalent of acquiring slaves); by eating the heart of a brave man, I acquire his courage; by eating a totem animal, I acquire the divine substance the totem animal symbolizes.[20]

Incorporation of a similar nature can be witnessed in the world of goods, where consumers desire the qualities of a product, brand or lifestyle and attempt to incorporate it through the process of consumption.

Affordable props are often purchased to assist in this process, particularly in the case of exclusive brands. These props may include Ferrari T-shirts, Louis Vuitton scarves, Alessi corkscrews, Porsche baseball caps or even a pair of Issey Miyake socks. The consumer desire for financially unattainable lifestyles often provokes this mode of incorporation through some pretty tenuous associations. When speaking of post-modern culture in *Symbolic Exchange and Death*, French social theorist Jean Baudrillard describes a contemporary detachment from reality toward a fabricated, and deeply abstracted, culture of signs. Baudrillard describes this process of reality fabrication as *simulation*, rendering McDonald's a simulation of convenience and Nike a simulation of streetwise independence. According to Baudrillard, consumption is motivated by a need for the simulation, rather than physical products themselves.

It is obstructive to perceive consumption as an isolated event or, perhaps, a split second happening that occurs when products are purchased: consumption is an unfolding process through which the external meanings and values as signified by objects are internalized by the consumer through engagement and subsequent familiarity. Sociologist Pasi Falk claims that consumption is a 'transformative and transcendent process of the appropriation and conversion of meaning'.[21] It is this process of appropriation and conversion that we as designers need to address, as it is through this process that strong connections between people and things are forged.

As discussed earlier, the consumption of material artefacts is largely motivated by the need to designate one's own particular being – matter serves to illustrate our values, beliefs and choices as an individual within an unstable and ever evolving societal mass. 'People acquire and own things to give expression to who they are and to show what group of people they feel they belong to.'[22] This self-defining mode of material engagement provides a mirror that casts brief existential reflections, through which we may both experience and evaluate our own individual life progress. Though a seemingly simplistic rationale for an issue of such apparent complexity, this single principle may well provide the very core of what drives the take-up and subsequent destruction of matter. In these instances, the desire to discard and replace is roused the moment objects lose their ability to effectively portray an individual's particular being; the complex assemblage of values and beliefs that collectively distinguish us as individuals are constantly changing, while the matter we deploy to portray these values and beliefs is relatively frozen in time. This indicates that it is merely a question of time before the majority of our material possessions begin to fall behind. Simply put, when the products we own reflect desirable and up-to-date reflections of our existence, they get to stay, while products that don't, do not.

Mapping need

To assist further comprehension, human needs may be mapped in several ways, initially by crudely polarizing them in two distinct categories consisting of innate needs and acquired needs. Innate needs are physiological, and include needs such as the need for shelter, food and oxygen, whereas acquired needs are psychological and may include needs, for example, such as the desire for prestige, status, friendship and social recognition. The distinction between physiological needs and psychological needs is useful and assists greatly in the entry-level comprehension of consumer motivation. This fairly crude opposition created between life-threatening and life-enhancing needs is often discussed in terms of need and want: to need water but to want Coca-Cola. Yet, this sets up an unhelpful opposition as all forms of desire – from the whimsical to the life threatening – are motivated primarily by need. For example, making friends, joining a collectors club, interacting with other people or consuming branded products are all behaviours motivated largely by the social need for affiliation. In contrast, obscure tastes in music, wild hairstyles or the purchasing of quirky products such as the Volkswagen (VW) Beetle are more likely to be motivated by the ego's need for a distinct sense of individuality as separate from the wider society.

Classifications between need and want are frequently concocted as a means of adopting the moral high ground. For example, when a vacuum cleaner breaks beyond repair it is considered morally acceptable to need a new one; yet, it would be perceived as immoral to own 2, 3 or maybe even 20 vacuum cleaners. These moral judgements are founded on the fragile premise that you only need one; yet, in the less developed world people survive perfectly fine without any at all, so whose concept of necessity are these moral guidelines based upon?

Maslow's hierarchy of needs

Twentieth-century American psychologist and philosopher Abraham Maslow categorizes all human need – regardless of moral judgement – within a simple pyramidal structure consisting of five hierarchical levels. Known as *Maslow's hierarchy of needs*, his theoretical model provides a comprehensive road map to human motivation. Maslow defines five levels of human need. These consist of *physiological needs*, such as water, food and breathable oxygen; *safety and security needs*, such as shelter, stability and a safe place in which to live; *social needs*, which may include companionship, tenderness and, perhaps, a sense of belonging; *ego needs*, which regularly include the need for prestige, status and positive self-esteem; and *self-actualization needs*, such as the successful accomplishment of personal goals.

Maslow's theoretical model facilitates the lucid comprehension of some fairly complex phenomena, and subsequently enjoys varied professional usage, from complex psychotherapy techniques to punchy direct marketing. The key premise underpinning Maslow's theory is that some needs take precedence over others, and they may therefore be organized within a hierarchical structure. For example, thirst is attended to before hunger, hunger is dealt with prior to safety, and safety comes way before companionship, tenderness and belonging. Maslow categorizes need within five navigable levels, stating that once the needs of a specific level are satisfied we proceed upward to the next.

In the comfortable developed world, the satisfaction of physiological needs, and safety and security needs is practically a given. This concentrates remaining human need within the other three levels; therefore, developed world consumer motivation is primarily driven by social, ego and self-actualizing need.

The crisis of individual evolution

'The only thing that does not change is that everything changes.'[23] Life is transient – never fixed – always in a state of continual evolutionary flux. As Earth steadily evolves, tides of biomass ebb and flow to its changing rhythms, from the sluggish adaptation of physiological evolution, to the more ephemeral cadence of social change. Caught in the hook of constant transience, the biosphere itself exists in an ageless state of perpetual rotation, rebirth and renewal. Whether the fleeting life cycle of a butterfly, the intensity and quality of sunlight or the slow tidal erosion of coastlines, we inhabit an amorphous world in which absolutely nothing is fixed. Even the Earth's gravitational pressure is believed to fluctuate marginally in reactance to universal variants. Transience weaves the very fabric of existence, providing both physical and metaphysical nourishment to all things on Earth. The only constant state on this planet, therefore, is that of change, and this is the way it has always been.

When speaking of evolution, most people recount the work of 19th-century British naturalist Charles Darwin, conjuring up images of primitive apes evolving into hairy bipedal Neanderthals who, in turn, evolve into smooth-skinned *Homo sapiens* consumers. Though laced with a distinctly Western linearity, Darwin's theory outlines the most common perception of human evolution today. His theory – illustrated most clearly in his revolutionary work entitled *On the Origin of Species* written in 1859 – provides a macro illustration in which the transformative process of natural selection drives the evolutionary progress of nature. Darwin's theory is of particular anthropological interest as it places all species within a temporal context and, in so doing, signposts both the origins and possible futures of any given species on Earth.

While Darwinian evolution may only be noticeable over several generations, other forms of evolution that occur far more swiftly are also taking place. On a psychological and psychosocial level, human evolution occurs on a daily, perhaps even hourly, basis. After all, we are continually growing and evolving – both as individuals and as a societal mass – and therefore may be described as existing within a similarly linear evolutionary timeline of perpetual growth and change. The nature of this kind of psychosocial evolution, however, yields even greater complexity, as it is both metaphysical and precariously random. It also lacks the rational singularity of natural selection due to its cross-contaminative social nature; we feed off each other, and grow in reactance to the unpredictable and random experiences that we encounter through our daily lives.

Flocking behaviour

Any human society is cybernetic; therefore, individual evolution will undoubtedly cross-pollinate with the wider perceptions of society at large. Studies from the Nomura Research Institute (NRI) suggest 'the consumption-related inclination of Japanese people very much resembles the flight patterns of a flock of birds'.[24] The NRI mapped the flocking behaviour of birds in an attempt to gain further understanding of the societal influence over consumer motivation. They subsequently streamed the birds' behaviour under three key principles:

1. A bird flies towards any large concentration of birds.
2. A bird flies at the same speed and direction of other birds.
3. A bird keeps its distance from nearby birds or barriers that come too close.

Just as a bird determines its actions on the basis of the three principles cited above by only watching the movements of other birds, Japanese consumers similarly keep an eye on what is happening around them and make decisions in accordance with the three basic values.[25]

Anyone familiar with the crowded Saturday afternoon shuffle along Oxford Street in London (UK) will no doubt agree that these theories may also be applicable to consumers who are not of Japanese descent. Furthermore, shared societal values shape and influence all individuals to render their version of individuality a simple abstraction – or adaptation – of the prevailing social norm:

> Seeking shelter, for example, essentially means the inclination to buy brand-name goods with the aim of seeking the approval and support of others. Similarly, pursuing fashion means the desire to stay abreast of what others are doing, while adhering to specific features caters to the pride of demonstrating one's uniqueness by purchasing goods that are slightly different from those owned by others.[26]

There can therefore be no such reality as an individual separate from society, just as there can be no societal mass without the presence of individuals. Indeed, the utopian myth of absolute individuality lurks deep within the consumer psyche; yet, it is just that, a utopian myth.

Beating down the wilderness

With the cognition of each emotion, sense and thought follows an autonomous reconfiguration of the self. Each new experience modifies us in some finite way, ensuring continual evolution and adaptation. Despite the accumulation of knowledge and experience so often attributed to the ageing process, it is seldom welcomed. The onset of age is often perceived as a debilitating phenomenon; whether the first grey hair, the rotting timbers in the attic or the erosion of a sandstone riverbank, transience antagonizes the human desire for mastery over all things by reminding us of our fleeting impermanence on this Earth. 'Human consciousness arose but a minute before midnight on the geological clock. Yet we mayflies try to bend an ancient world to our purposes, ignorant perhaps of the messages buried in its long history.'[27] For centuries, the human species has somewhat ignorantly striven to isolate itself from nature's decaying realm. Many researchers are beginning to suspect that 'we shall continue to have a worsening ecologic crisis until we reject the Christian axiom that nature has no reason for existence save to serve man'.[28] Furthermore, it is notable that 'the word "wilderness" occurs approximately 300 times in the Bible, and all its meanings are derogatory'.[29] This clearly indicates an early Western disapproval of natural systems, the anthropocentrism of which must be both learned from and, ultimately, surpassed. It is also worthy of note that to name nature both objectifies it and isolates it as a separate thing that somehow differs from regular life as experienced day to day.

As the Hindu proverb states: no physician is really good before he has killed one or two patients. We as a post-modern society have made some grave errors, and now it is time to learn from them. 'For 200 years we've been conquering Nature. Now we're beating it to death.'[30] Parks and gardens illustrate the extent to which we are prepared to live with nature today. They provide us with a subordinate muse, a controlled and manicured rendering of the natural world to be enjoyed on free weekends or long balmy summer evenings. However, there is a manufactured linearity underlying an avenue of poplar trees or a crescent mooned rockery that is symptomatic of the human desire to control and manipulate all life on Earth. In this light we can see that wilderness is nature at work and play, whereas 'a lawn is Nature under totalitarian rule'.[31]

Doggedly pursuing the dream of an enhanced durable world has enabled us to fabricate a plateau of material immunity; durable metals, polymers and composite materials have enabled us to construct this synthetic 'futurescape'. Immune to the glare of biological decay, these materials grossly outlive our desire for them, and so the illusion of control bares its first predicament: waste. Moreover, in desperately beating down the wildness of this chaotic world, we pinned things down and categorized them within rigid rules, formulaic principles, theoretical structures, mathematical systems and a host of other regulatory systems. In so doing we also created a cage-like world of predefined rules that now serve to cripple us through their own rigid inability to adapt with changing times. 'No theory ever agrees with all the facts in its domain; yet it is not always the theory that is to blame. Facts are constituted by older ideologies, and a clash between facts and theories may be proof of progress.'[32]

In creating order we simply increased the likelihood of disorder, and the rapid deterioration of the biosphere provides living testimony to this single contradiction. The current model of developed world production and consumption is fundamentally incompatible with natural systems; humans are moody, temperamental and erratic, which lends a peculiarity to the current model of design and manufacturing – which, in comparison, is a monosyllabic drone of mass manufactured monotony.

Obsolescence

What alternatives does this situation present to the consumer other than to hit the high street and seek stimulation elsewhere, only to be seduced by a newer version, fully charged with potentially obsolete meaning that, in time, will succumb to an identical fate? 'Some products are discarded before they are physically worn out or are technically superseded because their design is out of fashion or inappropriate to changed circumstances.'[33] When objects befall disuse in this manner we begin to see an alternative to the conventional model of obsolescence, in which goods are nullified by substantial shifts in technology, format or other operational protocol. Rather, obsolescence is also a consumer-side issue driven by the failure of products to quench the human thirst for new, fresh experiences. We outgrow what was once great; we become familiar to the greatness and, as we acclimatize to it, our expectations increase. The newly evolved self becomes impatient with that which – in evolutionary terms – holds it back; affection is immediately withdrawn and empathy subsequently fades. Thus, our initial adoring perception of the static in time product rapidly transforms into the resentment of a past that is now very much obsolete.

'Consuming has ambiguous qualities: it relieves anxiety, because what one has cannot be taken away; but it also requires one to consume ever more, because previous consumption soon loses its satisfactory character.'[34] These phenomena of individual evolution and the outgrowing of products have intensely destructive implications for the sustainability of consumerism; one-way evolutionary growth will only lead to the superseding of the other. In these cases, a total metaphoric consumption occurs that leaves objects with nothing more to offer their newly evolved users. For users at this juncture, products become nothing more than worthless husks of their former selves. To avoid such wasteful obsolescence, products must mutually evolve alongside users, sustaining value by revealing their true beauty only through the slow passing of time.

The deflowering gaze of familiarity

Consumption may be viewed as a process in which we attempt to know, familiarize and, ultimately, outgrow the wonders of artefacts. In 1943, French novelist and playwright Jean Paul Sartre referred to this destructive mode of knowledge-seeking as *deflowering*. In his classic existential work entitled *Being and Nothingness*, Sartre states: 'To have seen through and therefore know is to deflower the entity.'[35] The uptake of products is partially motivated by this notion of deflowering, as we consume the unknown in order to demystify and familiarize. Waste, therefore, is as much a part of the consumption experience as are purchase and use since it is evolution made tangible. Evolving objects and experiences would scupper consumers' attempts to deflower them by adopting a restless state of everlasting evolutionary growth to ensure that they always remain one step ahead of the user.

The developmental relationships that occur between owners and their pets are demonstrative of this phenomenon; after all, how often do dogs become obsolete? Phillip Gregory of BS Technologies' Silicon Valley Research Lab states that one of the greatest pleasures of owning a dog is its stupidity. 'What greater joy is there than throwing a ball and watching him run after it until he realizes that you never let go? Or the way you can say anything at all to him, and as long as you use the right tone, he'll wag his tail regardless.'[36] Modern products seriously lack this kind of character and allure; they are too smart and precise, removing all possible surprise, mystery and, perhaps above all, charm from the process of engaging with them.

The mirror stage

As mentioned earlier, we as individuals are constantly evolving: but for what reasons, and why do we always move forward? What is it that we so desperately strive to evolve away from? In 1949, French psychoanalyst Jacques Lacan developed a theory that pointed to the origins of this common behavioural phenomenon, which he referred to as *the mirror stage*. The mirror stage depicts a developmental stage observable in infants aged roughly between 6 to 18 months. During this developmental period, infants are said to be able to recognize themselves in the mirror as a whole and separate entity, instead of the fragmented movements and undefined boundaries between self and other – baby and mother, especially – which have constituted their experiential world up to this point. Lacan's theory demonstrates that infants have desires to see themselves as an *I*, a separate entity with equally separate ideas and practices. Lacan states that once experienced, this craving for individuality and separatism will remain active until death. Furthermore, the vision reflected in the mirror comes at a time when infants possess little motor control over their bodies. The mirror portrays the *I* as an imperfect self – a mirage of partial control – laced with flaws and imperfections. 'The clumsiness witnessed has the effect in man of an organic insufficiency in his natural reality.'[37] This event later manifests a permanent sense of being imperfect, while constantly looking forward to achieving perfection, and we thus spend the present creating the future to outdistance the past.

Ego

Meaningful connotations are as powerfully dangerous as they are complex; they set up demanding expectations within the consumer at both rational and emotional levels. A consumer will identify powerfully with meanings that support their own perception of themselves. This closes them off to contrasting meanings that could be said to challenge or devolve that fragile self.

Freud attributed this behavioural foundation to the origin of ego, which according to both Lacan and Freud exists as an accumulation of aspirations and dreams. The ego maintains false appearances, portraying an aggregate self-image of coherence, completeness and success. 'The ego is thus always an inauthentic agency, functioning to conceal a disturbing lack of unity.'[38] Consumption therefore assists the construction of a desired identity through which the self and other may be subsequently defined, constructing a desired identity through which users may mediate their particular values and motivations as an individual within society. The consumption of heavy signifiers such as iMacs and Gucci bags fits neatly into this rationale, shedding further light on the human desire to surround oneself with what might best be described as meaningful matter. When discussing emotional attachment, Freud claims that, 'At the height of being in love, the boundary between ego and object threatens to melt away. Against all the evidence of his senses, a man who is in love declares that *I* and *you* are one, and is prepared to behave as if it were a fact.'[39] This notion gives strong clues to the origins of our desire to consume and surround ourselves with meaningful matter. 'The ego is constituted by an alienating identification, based on an initial lack of completeness in the body and nervous system.'[40]

As a materialist society, we commonly represent and mediate the fabric of our egos through objects as opposed to language. Verbal communication is insufficiently equipped to provide us with an absolute identity as other people also use the words we use; we do not own them and 'the words do not belong to us'.[41] In contrast, objects stimulate the ego's desire to conceal our private insecurities, as their ambiguous meaning may be interpreted in a profundity of ways. Thus, reacting to the failure of speech in designating our particular being, we employ objects to do the talking for us. Interestingly, substantial evidence from the research fields of psychoanalysis and linguistics indicates that the more users experience alienation in speech, the more they will separate themselves from it, to find refuge in the silent yet meaningful embrace of objects.

Today, the symbolic world varies tremendously according to social groupings and evolves over time. Furthermore, it is not only language that changes with the advancements of society, but also the meanings that these words signify. Just as in the case of mass-manufactured objects, language, too, is in possession of evolutionary characteristics and is thus of a similar instability. For example, while the word *oasis* once meant an isolated area of vegetation within a barren environment, now it denotes the name of a rock music band, while 'most people, asked recently in a survey what they associated with the word Madonna, replied sex, not the Virgin Mary'.[42]

Empathy has a lifespan

Most products are capable of creating even a small amount of empathy at the point of purchase; from this point on, however, product longevity is soberly dependent upon the sustainability of that empathy. Like everything in this unstable world, empathy, too, has a lifespan, governed in this case by the type of relationship that is evident between the user and the object. Waste, therefore, is a symptom of expired empathy, a kind of failed relationship that leads to the dumping of one by the other. As in so many other relationships – particularly inter-human pair bonding – when the adoration and meaning fades, the original pair bond weakens. Another fresh bonding urge is then motivated, often resulting in the acquisition of another; the original relationship is superseded and the partner is rendered obsolete. Mutual evolution will effectively transcend obsolescence of this nature by successfully carrying the partnership well beyond its passionate early stages. Desire for fresh reflections of the ever evolving self also manifests itself through a resentment of the stale. In defining consumption as a meaning-seeking process, you automatically reframe the very idea of waste; waste becomes a symptom of expired meaning – a statement from a newly evolved self:

> Our existence has no foundation on which to rest except the transient present. Thus, its form is essentially unceasing motion, without any possibility of that

repose which we continually strive after. It resembles the course of a man running down a mountain who would fall over if he tried to stop and can stay on his feet only by running on; or a pole balanced on the tip of the finger; or a planet which would fall into the sun if it ever ceased to plunge irresistibly forward. Thus, existence is typified by unrest.[43]

In evolutionary terms, to consume is to aspire, and to waste is to stride forth in triumph. Therefore, the origin of the ecological crisis we face appears to lurk deep within a single, yet profoundly universal, inconsistency. Consumer aspirations continually evolve, whereas products are hopelessly frozen in time. As we consume further meaning, our ideals change and shift, as does our experience base upon which we found a sense of self. The consumer quest for meaning continues as it always will; however, until products embody a transient flexibility to shift and adapt in sync with us, we will always be adding to an immense landfill of transferred matter whose only crime was a failure to keep up.

Metaphysical versus physical

Various notions of product life orbit the creative sphere and have done so for some time. In the majority of cases, objects are supposedly rendered durable via the specification of resilient materials, repairable technologies and robust design engineering. This somewhat cautious approach to product life-extension adorns products with physically enduring properties in pre-emption of their rough lives to come. Yet, this objective model of durability also places pressure on the biosphere: once they have been discarded, products born of this mindset become acutely counterproductive. Landfills bloat with strata upon strata of durable goods, slowly living out their tough robust existences beneath 10,000 tonnes of likeminded scrap. It therefore appears clear that there is little point designing physical durability into consumer goods if the consumer has no desire to keep them.

Few would contest that the principal endeavour of durability is to optimize the functional life of objects. Yet, as any cat skinner will testify, there is always more than one way to achieve an end. Thus far, the creative methodologies addressing design for durability possess monism, single-minded approaches that attend to the physical, cosmetic survival of artefacts. In these somewhat superficial scenarios, durability is distinguished purely by a product's physical endurance, whether cherished or discarded; engineers therefore slap each other's backs in triumph as fully functioning hairdryers emerge from a five-year landfill hiatus. Is this durable product design, or simply the designing of durable waste? In addition, product failure is essentially characterized by blown circuits, stress fractures and a host of other technical and physical glitches; in attending solely to physical ageing, designers overlook numerous invaluable metaphysical renderings of durability. As a creative industry, it is vital that we break away from the physical and begin to understand more about the sustainability of empathy, meaning, desire and other metaphysical factors that influence the duration of product life – nurturing a new and enlightened wave of design built on a deeper understanding of how consumers create and sustain attachments within this overabundant material world.

Chapter summary

Material consumption is driven by complex motivations and is about far more than just the acquisition of newer, shinier things. It is an endless personal journey toward the ideal or desired self that, by its very nature, becomes a process of incremental destruction.

· ·

Ecological procrastination could be likened to the experience of delaying a visit to the dentist. Though perfectly aware that each day brings further discomfort, the decaying tooth goes unattended, ensuring that the inevitable operation will be far more dreadful when it does eventually arrive.

· ·

We are consumers of meaning and not matter; products provide a chassis that signify the meanings to be consumed. We transfer resources into products that – in a sense – provide us with existential mirrors, allowing us to view and experience our dreams and desires in real time.

· ·

Material consumption operates on a range of experiential layers; consumers mine these layers, unearthing meaningful content as they steadily excavate deeper into the semiotic core of an object. Designers must weave intricacy amongst the layers of an object in order to optimize the sustainability of this meaningfulness.

. . . .

New needs emerge the moment old needs are met, thus nurturing the infinite sequence of desire and destruction that is so characteristic of the modern world.

. . . .

The notion of meaning is highly context specific: the meaning of a rat in a pet shop differs greatly from that of the same rat in a restaurant kitchen. Meaning can thus be loosely directed by designers, but never fully controlled.

. . . .

Doggedly pursuing the dream of a technologically enhanced and physically durable world has enabled us to fabricate a plateau of material immunity. Durable metals, polymers and composite materials have enabled us to construct this synthetic 'futurescape'; immune to the glare of biological decay, these materials grossly outlive our desire for them and so the illusion of control bares its first predicament: waste.

. . . .

Conventional wisdom dictates that goods are nullified by substantial shifts in technology, format or other operational protocol; however, obsolescence is also a consumer side issue driven by the failure of products to quench the human thirst for new, fresh experiences.

. . . .

The uptake of products is partially motivated by the notion of deflowering; we consume the unknown in order to demystify and familiarize. Modern products lack character; they are too smart and precise, removing all possible surprise, mystery and, perhaps above all, charm from the process of engagement.

. . . .

The ego exists as an accumulation of aspirations and dreams, maintaining false appearances and portraying an aggregate self-image of coherence, completeness and success.

. . . .

As a materialist society, we commonly represent and communicate the fabric of our egos through objects as opposed to language.

. . . .

Most products are capable of creating even a small amount of empathy at the point of purchase; from this point on, however, product lifespans depend upon the sustainability of that empathy. Waste, therefore, could be seen as a symptom of expired empathy: a failed relationship that led to the dumping of one by the other.

. . . .

In human pair bonding, when empathy fades the original bond weakens. Another fresh bonding urge is motivated, resulting in the acquisition of another; the original relationship is rendered obsolete.

. . . .

Various notions of product life orbit the creative sphere and have done so for some time. In the majority of cases, objects are supposedly rendered durable via the specification of resilient materials, repairable technologies and robust design engineering. Landfills bloat with strata upon strata of durable goods, slowly living out their tough robust existences beneath 10,000 tonnes of likeminded scrap.

. . . .

There is little point designing physical durability into consumer goods if consumers have no desire to keep them.

. . . .

In attending solely to physical ageing, designers overlook numerous metaphysical renderings of durability. As a creative industry it is vital that we break away from the physical and begin to understand more about the sustainability of empathy, meaning, desire and other metaphysical factors that influence the duration of product life.

A toolbox of ideas

See beyond the physical: it is important to see beyond the physical, attending equally to the meanings that a product signifies. Essentially, consumers acquire meanings, not objects; objects simply provide a way of perceiving the meaning. Furthermore, try to gauge through scenario-building to what degree these meanings are sustainable and how they might evolve over time, if at all.

. . . .

Relinquish control: avoid over-programming the product semantic to ensure that sufficient space is left for the inclusion of the user's psyche. The ambiguous qualities that manifest as a result of designing in this way increase the likelihood of chance discoveries, randomness and intimacy, which, in turn, greatly facilitate the nurture of subject–object empathy.

· ·

Keep the magic alive: make sure that a few cards are concealed up the object's sleeve; if a product relinquishes all meaning in a single fleeting glance – experientially – consumers have nowhere left to go. By designing products to patiently deliver a series of future discoveries and revelatory happenings, the life of an object is dramatically increased as users remain captivated in anticipation of the next event.

· ·

Meaning is context specific: utilize the instability of meaning as an agent of chance. Object meanings change significantly in relation to their contextual surroundings; designers must embrace this unpredictable quality as it enables objects to radiate multiple personalities, which scupper the user's attempts to out-know them.

chapter three

attachments with objects

The dawn of material culture

Ample historic evidence exists to suggest that even earlier versions of our present selves may have fabricated some form of material culture: a culture riddled with such familiar sounding traits as interactivity, symbolism, inter-societal comparing and strong emotional attachments to one's material possessions. Yet, despite the extensive archives of research that are available to us today, it still remains uncertain as to how, when and – perhaps more interestingly – why our species developed such a materialist orientation.

Earlier forms of material culture embodied an animistic appreciation of the physical world not too different from the way we perceive it today. Animism of this nature was prevalent among primitive peoples, with the 'belief that inanimate objects and the phenomena of nature are endowed with personal life or a living soul'.[1] Examples of this might include feathers believed to be sacred, pebbles that could heal the sick or a tiger bone possessing the strength and vigour of the deceased animal. All of these items could be owned and thus afforded the owner with their signified properties, in a similar way that a Prada bag might afford elegant sophistication today.

Archaeologists have made numerous findings that point to the prehistoric origins of material culture. Hunter-gatherers of the Upper Palaeolithic period of the late Pleistocene epoch left a rich legacy of cave paintings, tools, body adornment and a wealth of other material artefacts. The Kenyan site of *Enkapune Ya Muto* – Twilight Cave – has turned up beads made from ostrich eggshells, which date back approximately 40,000 years. It is believed that:

> … their maker shaped the crude, circular pieces from fragments of ostrich eggshell, thinning each one and drilling a hole through the centre. Many of them broke before they were finished. An unknown Stone Age artisan spent hours crafting these decorations rather than searching for food, tending children or making tools.[2]

Anthropology professor Richard G. Klein believes the eggshell beads and other such findings indicate the very dawn of material culture. Klein states that:

> … with their new sense of aesthetic, they made the first clearly identifiable art. And they freed themselves to wander beyond the local watering hole – setting the stage for long-distance trade – with contrivances like canteens and the delicately crafted eggshell beads, which may have functioned as 'hostess gifts' to cement goodwill with other clans.[3]

Klein maintains that these events have influenced the development of the human species more than anything else in recent times:

> Forget about upheavals like the Russian and French Revolutions, which produced mere changes of costume. Forget about the construction of the first cities or the introduction of the internal combustion engine. The revolution that made the biggest difference occurred on the Savannah of East Africa roughly 45,000 years ago.[4]

The cultural big bang

Most anthropologists agree that about half a millennium ago, human creativity somehow skyrocketed in a kind of cultural big bang. The reasons for this genesis are currently unknown, though speculative theories abound. Some claim that 'humans suddenly crossed a threshold of creativity after a long, slow build-up in population',[5] implying that it was only a matter of time before things got interesting. Others state that 'a radical population boom set off a maelstrom of competition between groups, inspiring rapid innovation'.[6] When discussing the development of Neolithic material culture Russian anthropologist D. V. Gerasirnov claims that 'changes of pottery depended more on a changes of fashion caused by contacts with neighbour tribes'.[7] We can therefore see that the social malaise of continual comparison and competition was rampant even in these relatively primitive times.

Although the ways in which we manipulate matter today may have developed beyond recognition, our existential and frequently animistic utilization of material objects remains unchanged:

> According to Marx, the things we make ourselves acquire all the characteristics of ancient fetishes. They are endowed with spiritual qualities that we don't understand and they are ruling us instead of serving our needs. Marx considers this a reversal of the normal subject–object relationship.[8]

Similar logic reversals occurred in the transition from modernism to post-modernism. 'In the [1950s] modernism ended with contemporary style, when the way was paved for pop design and, eventually, post-modernism, some 20 years later. From then on not the function of the object became the key issue, but its meaning.'[9] In direct contrast with function-oriented modernist methodologies, the creative endeavours of post-modernism place meaning way before function:

> Products become icons, symbols or signs. They do not even need to be durable anymore, as they did for modernists. This indicates that to post-modernism matter is even less important. Objects are seen as embodiments of meaning, and it is from this perspective that they have to be designed. The platonic anti-

materialism is evident. Post-modern designers are not primarily concerned with things, but with ideas.[10]

Towards individualism and materialism

The utilization of matter as a signifier of meaning is anything but a modern preoccupation, driven by primal urges that have lurked deep within us for aeons. Materialism, however, developed incrementally by somehow managing to stay within the carrying capacities of the natural environment. Furthermore, materialistic lifestyles were compatible with tribal life and did not obstruct pair bonding, friendships, intimacy or other vital sociological functioning. It is worth noting that 'the history of consumerism shows that there is a relationship between changes in culture and changes in consumption patterns. It shows further that these changes move away from communal values toward individualism and materialism.'[11] It was therefore not until very recently that the darker side of material culture pulled into view.

During recent years:

> … there has been a move away from both intrapersonal and interpersonal relationships to a new mode of relations. The direction of this move has been to the surface. The resulting mode of relating is best described as extropersonal. This term is meant to describe an outwardly personal relationship. This outward focus denotes a relatedness with the surface or exterior, as distinguished from the mind or spirit. [12]

Furthermore, 'the extropersonal relationship is the prominent type of relationship today, and results from the pervasiveness of consumerism in our society'.[13] This can also be seen clearly in cultural historian Philip Cushman's notion of the empty self 'characterized by a pervasive sense of personal emptiness that uses consumption as a means for filling up, and where loneliness is embodied as emotional hunger'.[14] Desire to engage in meaningful relationships with material objects may therefore emerge from this emptiness, existing as a futile effort to re-centre oneself.

Today, communal life is fragmented over countless relationships, not with one another, but with objects, brands and other designed experiences. Somewhere during the last 100 years we learned to find refuge outside the species, in the silent embrace of manufactured objects. Why we migrated in this particular direction no one is quite sure; most believe that we were seduced by the speed and streamlined efficacy of a modern manufactured world. Many blame the mid 1900s industrial revolution for today's overabundant production, consumption and subsequent environmental decay, stating that such enhanced production capabilities were beyond our control and was like giving a Ferrari to a four-year old. Others are beginning to suspect that the drivers underpinning modern materialism are non-economic, reflecting a disturbing lack of wholeness within the self.

Researcher Fritz M. Brunner believes that:

> … besides political and economical factors, the absence of spirituality has also led to the growth of consumerism. Without a figurehead in their lives to guide them spiritually, people have no sense of direction. Instead, they seek solace in material things and procure them not because they need them, but that they have to fill that void of emptiness within their souls by spending on themselves.[15]

Similarly, in the creative industries, it is accepted that we are here today because of the symbolic power of objects in signifying desirable identities and consumable destinies. Realistically, it was most likely a cocktail of these and several other theories that came together, like a mid air collision some time during the 20th century to create the grossly transient, fast-food model of materialism that we fumble through today.

Desire and disappointment

In this oversaturated world of people and things, durable attachments with objects are seldom witnessed. Most products deliver a predictable diatribe of information, which quickly transforms wonder into drudgery. Although emotional attachments are not extinct just yet, durable connections between users and their mass manufactured counterparts are very rarely forged:

> Engagement has become a rare commodity now that the great emancipatory
> narratives have fallen silent and designers have become individualistic and
> realistic. Our age is one of total relativism. We lack a common purpose. Design
> has become a practice without content, geared towards surface appearance
> and financial success.[16]

Perhaps through our unhealthy modern-day fixations with technological
contemporaneousness, the surface characteristics of products and their
ability to quickly generate sales, we have inadvertently designed away the
more poetic and enduring characteristics of material culture. In so doing,
we formulated a transient and unstable platform of goods upon which the
hopes and dreams of users must precariously balance.

Consumers are unable to develop and sustain attachments with
objects lacking such characteristics as the objects do not possess the
diversity and pluralism of character required to healthily sustain enquiry. The
ensuing sequence of desire and disappointment that follows comes with a
distinctly checkout bleeping regularity, and thus provides a vital cornerstone
of the capitalist empire. It should be noted here that the ecological crisis
resulting from the excess of material culture is almost exclusively geared
around the economic interests of the developed world. 'Globally, the 20
per cent of the world's people in the highest-income countries account for
86 per cent of total private consumption expenditures – the poorest 20
per cent a minuscule 1.3 per cent.'[17] A gross inequity exists between the
economically developed and undeveloped nations of the world; yet, the
environmental problems caused by excessive material consumption affect
all under the sun:

> We consume a variety of resources and products today, having moved beyond
> basic needs to include luxury items and technological innovations to try to
> improve efficiency. Such consumption beyond minimal and basic needs is not
> necessarily a bad thing in and of itself, as throughout history we have always
> sought to find ways to make our lives a bit easier to live.[18]

However, in the developed North human relatedness with the material
world has become both excessive and unstable. Products are mindlessly

cast aside to make way for newer and fresher experiences with shocking regularity. Perhaps due to the normalcy of innovation, material culture has adopted an expendable and sacrificial persona. Today, an edgy sense of instability surrounds contemporary material culture, nurtured by continual change to render its offspring fleeting, transient and replaceable orphans of circumstance. Tonight, a flat-screen Trinitron TV lies face down, discarded like a spent cigarette, in the wet space between pavement and road; an abandoned refrigerator stands outcast in a dark suburban alleyway, while an Apple Macintosh from the beige era garnishes a skip filled with construction rubble.

The honeymoon period

The passionate early stages of a subject–object relationship could be described as a honeymoon period, a period of intense synergy within which everything is new, interesting and the consumption of one another is feverish. Honeymoon periods are by their very nature short lived and must, ultimately, give way to the inevitable onset of normalcy. In human-to-human scenarios, the transition from honeymoon to normal daily life is ordinarily smooth and occurs without too many problems. This is largely because the expectations of most newlyweds are reasonably well synchronized with reality, and therefore disappointment is seldom nurtured by the transition. In most cases, disappointment may be characterized quite simply by a real-time imbalance between expectation and reality. Therefore, the utopian futures promised by most products at the point of purchase set up grossly unrealistic expectations within consumers, and these expectations practically guarantee disappointment the moment honeymoon periods draw to a close. In consequence, emotional attachments with objects are generally fleeting and seriously lack qualitative substance. In the material world, transitions from honeymoon to daily life are anything but smooth and occur with an awakening jolt. In this context, it can be seen that the onset of normalcy sounds the death knell for most objects, and thus must be regarded as nothing less than the beginning of the end. During recent years, consumers have become serial honeymooners, and today subject–object relationships are less marriage, more one-night stand.

Modern consumers are short-distance runners, promiscuous debauchees who only stay for the getting-to-know-you period, when all is fresh, new and novel. In this way, it is clear to see that waste is nothing more than a symptom of a failed relationship, a failure that led to the dumping of the static one by the newly evolved other. As is so often witnessed in human pair-bonding relations, when adoration fades the original bond weakens. Fresh bonding urges are promptly motivated, resulting in the acquisition of another. Thus, the relationship is superseded and the original partner is rendered obsolete. In a sense we outgrow what was once great, feeling we no longer need them or, perhaps, could do better. We become familiar with their greatness and, as we acclimatize to it, our expectation of greatness itself subsequently increases. The newly evolved self soon becomes impatient with that which in evolutionary terms holds it back. Adoration rapidly mutates into a resentment of a past that is now outdated and obsolete. This common phenomenon of individual evolution and the out-growing of a product yield intensely destructive implications for the sustainability of consumerism. One-way polarized growth motivates a superseding of the static other, a kind of total metaphoric consumption that leaves the product with nothing else to offer the user.

What does this situation present to the consumer other than to seek stimulation elsewhere and hit the high street once more – only to be seduced by a newer and shinier version of the predecessor, which in time will certainly succumb to an identical fate? 'The human being is engaged, throughout his life span, in an unceasing struggle to differentiate himself increasingly fully, not only from his human, but also from his non-human environment.'[19] Consumerism and waste are at the mercy of a constant human search for fresh, current definitions of individuality. The contemporary model of capitalism feeds off this socially antagonistic mode of serial dissatisfaction. Physical objects are not the focus of our deep desires; they are merely tangible entities, which transport, package and render various meanings perceivable. In this respect, objects provide vehicles for the delivery of meaningful signifiers, and we engage faithfully and passionately with them, at first anyway.

From honeymoon to the daily grind

Objects capable of sustaining long-lasting relationships with consumers are rare. Most emotional attachments are withdrawn once the honeymoon period draws to a close. This is largely because the evolution that takes place is grossly polarized, occurring almost exclusively within the user.

In the made world, a relentless cycle of desire and disappointment is in progress. Products once loved and cherished by users fall out of favour with surprising regularity. As mentioned earlier, in most cases the withdrawal of emotional attachment and subsequent loss of empathy are caused by a noticeable discrepancy between actual and imagined realities. Consumers like to believe that this will be the last toaster they will ever need, or that a Dyson vacuum cleaner is going to put the oomph back into the daily grind we call life. Expectations are therefore unreasonably high, making the transition from honeymoon to daily life a harsh smack down to Earth. Users characterize this moment as disappointment, though to be accurate the real problem lies in the overly optimistic expectations of each user, while marketers and designers catalyse this common imbalance further. Products make claims that are hard to back up, promising the world to consumers from the safety of the shop window, bombarding consumers with a loud and colourful array of false claims.

Though short-term marketing edge may be acquired via this strategy, excessively raising expectations simply increases the likelihood of disappointment, sealing the inevitable fate of this future trash. Consumers acclimatize to stimulation quickly and demands subsequently increase. New situations quickly lose their sense of novelty as we gradually adapt to them; whether acclimatizing to the muggy humidity of Taipei, the frenzied busyness of Tokyo or the serene tranquillity of the English Lake District, normalcy slowly erodes away the jagged edges of newness, transforming unfamiliar sensations into known and familiar ones. In fact, our extraordinary ability in adapting to new situations possesses a degree of efficiency that is frequently counterproductive, particularly in terms of the ecological implications of consumerism.

Growing together

Most products within the current model of design are static, possessing non-evolutionary souls; we as users, on the other hand, are anything but static and exist within a restless state of continual adaptation and growth. The problems arising from this restlessness are also evident within the sustainability of inter-human relations, as synchronizing both the rate and nature of this constant evolutionary change is practically impossible; anomalies emerge between two previously well-synchronized people, and tension normally follows.

Most marriage guidance counsellors will confirm that poorly synchronized growth can lead to marital difficulties. One partner may outgrow the other, and soon they begin to feel as though they are somehow being held back. More often than not, both partners grow and evolve, but in radically different directions, often causing incompatibility, conflict and the eventual degeneration of empathy. Comfort may be sought in material consumption, as it is always us who outgrows, us who evolves, us who decides when enough is enough. 'Though it is not necessarily a good thing, some people clearly find the company of electronic products more satisfying than that of people.'[20] In the material world, when the adoration and empathy fades – as it almost always does – the original pair bond weakens and fresh bonding urges are motivated. The consumer eye begins to wander, dreaming of more desirable futures with newer models. Relationships at this juncture are quickly superseded, and due to the lack of empathy between subject and object, replacement occurs with the greatest of ease. The throughput of material and energy required to support this pattern of adulterous consumption is catastrophic in proportion, causing great devastation to the natural world. In contrast, it appears feasible that a relationship characterized by well-synchronized mutual evolution might assist in carrying subject–object partnerships beyond their passionate early stages. Relationships frequently break down as a result of under-stimulation experienced by either both, or one of two parties. An incompatibility of pace and direction of individual evolution is experienced, inducing sensations of frustration that can distance one partner from the other.

When discussing the longevity of emotional attachment, relationship counsellor John Gray – author of the international bestseller

Men Are from Mars, Women Are from Venus – describes relationships as
sporadic, deeply confusing and somewhat irregular. 'It is very common for
two people who are madly in love one day to hate each other or fight the
very next day. These sudden shifts are confusing; yet they are common.'[21]
Gray claims that these peaks and troughs are the result of unresolved
emotions lurking deep in the subconscious mind, and when we feel
empathy – or love – we tend to relax. It is at the moment of relaxation that
the unresolved emotions feel that it is safe to come to the surface.
'It is as though your unresolved feelings wait until you are feeling loved, and
then they come up to be healed.'[22] Pretty soon we begin to feel irritable,
critical and resentful of our partners, blaming them for these unwanted
emotions that seem to come from nowhere. Feelings such as these are not
only triggered by love, but can also be the consequence of other intense
emotional events in life, such as Christmas, birthdays or the new year.
Families and friends find these occasions treacherous to navigate without
conflict of some sort, and frequently fall foul of the repressed emotion
phenomenon.

Love

To speak of love as existing within the material domain conjures notions
of obscurity and fanaticism. Despite this, it cannot be ignored that the
emotional instability of humans provides a wild card element to the
development of attachments with objects. Furthermore, it appears clear
that the human development of empathic relationships with objects is
powerfully influenced by this characteristic instability. Designers must learn
to embrace human unpredictability before they can attempt to effectively
enrich and elongate subject–object engagement.

Today, most people are comfortable in the misguided belief that
love is an emotion exclusive to the human species. However, love is an
intrinsic facet of mainstream material culture and has been for some time.
Love interlaces the material fabric of one's life; whether it is the love of
a Renaissance painting, stewed apples and custard, a compact disc (CD)
reminiscent of old friends, or even the love of your new G5 Mac, love
abounds in both the made and unmade worlds. Designer Tony Brook
discusses a growing affection for his new found friend, the G5 Mac, stating:

> I'm not madly geeky as far as kit goes. Admittedly, I was thrilled with the Cinema Display and seduced by the ubiquitous iPod (full fat, not the wussy pastel iPod Lite). But my new G5 is a thing of rare beauty. It positively radiates. I have to confess to stroking it, though I haven't patted or talked to it, yet.[23]

The love that users develop for manufactured objects may not be the stuff of Mills and Boon; firstly, it lacks the two-way emotional exchange upon which love so desperately feeds and, secondly, it is a love incapable of mutual evolution and growth. The life expectancy of the love established between people and things is therefore limited and ordinarily fades once the gloss of newness has worn away. Indeed, the love between subject and object is oftentimes transient and is seldom eternal; then again, the same may be said of inter-human relations, which often portray equal degrees of instability and fragility that are not altogether different.

Occasionally, humans and objects hit it off to surprising degrees; as if by accident, strong empathic bonds are formed between subject and object, forging practically inseparable unions – a durable 'consumerscape' far beyond the ephemeral realm of serial honeymooning and adulterous consumption, from which soul mates triumphantly emerge. One notable example is an Australian man who felt such strong empathic bonds with his TV set that he actually married it:

> During the ceremony, he placed a gold wedding ring on top of the TV set and one on his finger. He even promised to 'love, honour, and obey' the product. One day it just occurred to him that his TV was the best companion he had ever had – he watched up to ten hours a day.[24]

This is, of course, a somewhat exceptional occurrence; however, our Aussie friend simply takes a common behavioural phenomenon one step further, or perhaps two steps?

Most people will admit to spending too much time in front of the TV, on the phone or plonked before a computer roaming expansive consumer portals such as eBay and Yahoo. Manufactured artefacts frequently receive the lion's share of our free time, often taking precedence over people in the battle for attention. Custom car enthusiasts often claim to spend more time with their automobile than with their immediate family. Despite the peculiarity of these anecdotes, they indicate that increased subject–object empathy has the potential to considerably elongate honeymoon periods in rich and emotionally resonant ways.

A streamlined world

Amidst the monotony of today's over-streamlined world, most consumer products are not designed to facilitate any great intensities of interaction; in consequence, the range of experiences delivered by artefacts born of this mindset are both restricted and short lived. Since the closing of the 20th century, users have found themselves increasingly sequestered from meaningful material engagements, unwittingly relegated to the role of button pushers – a passive audience who simply presses go, then stands back to watch as anonymous black boxes perform their magic. It may therefore be asserted that in terms of facilitating emotional attachment between users and objects, the current model of design is on an entirely different page.

Caroline Hummels of the Department of Industrial Design at Delft University of Technology expresses concern over the increasingly anonymous and experience-impoverished direction in which design appears to be currently heading. She draws our attention to this by recounting the rich emotional experience of interacting with an old record player:

> I cautiously removed the precious gramophone record from its cover and placed it on the turntable. With the no-static brush I carefully removed the hardly visible dust particles. I lifted up the arm, gently blew a bit of fluff from the needle and moved it smoothly above the record. After a last check, I carefully placed the needle in the groove. A soft tick, a cracking noise, and a few seconds later the beautiful voice of Mathilde Santing filled the room.[25]

Most of us are familiar with the experience of laying down vinyl, and the degree of care, focus and overall emotional involvement that this delicate process commands. In contrast, most of us are also familiar with the comparatively prosaic mode of engagement commanded by vinyl's younger brother, the CD, which may be viewed as an epoch-making development in acoustic innovation, but a significant step backwards in terms of the emotional experience that it generally delivers. Hummels further points out that 'the voice of Santing is now written on a silver disc, which is tucked inside a black box with several anonymous buttons'.[26] So often we see the endeavours of technological innovation deployed to hasten the process of interaction, and remove the decision-making process from increasingly alienated users.

Streamlined efficiency need not be at odds with rich interactive experiences, and the products we create to mediate emergent technologies need to embrace this ideology. The commercial model discussed here represents 'just one approach to product design, one genre, if you like, which offers a very limited experience. Like a Hollywood movie the emphasis is on easy pleasure and conformist values.'[27] Alternative product genres could emerge: genres that challenge, provoke and force cognitive enquiry; genres that sustain attachment by enabling layer upon layer of empathy to form, while providing the user with an endless profundity of rich and varied experience:

> Products could offer more complex and demanding aesthetic experiences if designers referred to this bizarre world of the 'infra-ordinary', where stories show that truth is indeed stranger than fiction, and prove that our experience of everyday life lived through conventional electronic products is aesthetically impoverished.[28]

Designing dependency

Dependency is frequently spoken of as an abnormal degree of reliance on something that is psychologically or physically habit-forming, such as coffee, chocolate, alcohol or narcotics. We may also hear dependency spoken of as a lack of independence or self-sufficiency, where specific needs are fulfilled through a reliance on other people or things, including a dependency on, for example, central heating, public transport, the National Health Service, parents or a best friend. More interestingly, dependencies commonly exist of which most of us are not consciously aware, such as our constant dependency on the Earth to sustain its gravitational pull, or on the ability of our bodies to maintain a healthy pH balance. These rudimentary dependencies are of particular interest as they serve to remind us that we are never completely in control of our lives, much as we would like to believe that we are. Finally, there is a flip side to dependency in which we are the entity being depended upon. In contrast to the aforementioned outgoing dependencies, this alternative rendering of incoming dependency may be likened to the needy reliance underpinning the love received by a master from their dog. It is this dependency and neediness that often bridges the void between otherwise separate entities to create a relationship, founded on the symbiotic exchange of reliance and need.

The importance of this point cannot be overemphasized, particularly in the context of subject–object relationships. Everyday objects that engage the senses in this way should not be taken for granted; their characteristics are not simply utilitarian or aesthetic. They invade our lives and literally depend upon our care and attention in order to survive. It is this co-dependency that gives rise to deep sensations of cohesion, attachment and, potentially, love. Most physical experiences create a modest sense of dependency, as they depend upon our care to survive. Even the most commonplace of products are dependent in some way or another – be it a mobile phone's dependency on recharging, a car's continual need for maintenance, a suede bag's protection from the weather or simply a paintbrush's yearning to be used, enabling its purpose to be fulfilled. Fundamental levels of dependency such as these have become so commonplace in contemporary material existence that most users are no longer aware of them. They therefore go largely unnoticed, transforming subject–object relations into the non-synergistic and ordinarily fugacious sequence of interactions so characteristic of modern times.

Tamagotchi

Previous research into attachment between subject and object through artificial intelligence scenarios has acquired quirkiness, focusing almost exclusively on the research and development of families of domestic robotics. These generally include digital pet simulations, such as Sony's AIBO, Bandai's Tamagotchi, or Hasbro's FURBY, which essentially seek to stimulate the parental urge that supposedly lurks within in each of us.

The nurturing of visceral and emotional attachments between users and objects is illustrated particularly well in the case of the Tamagotchi from Bandai. Tamagotchi was a Japanese concept resulting from an attempt to inject a sense of dependency into the digital product. First introduced in

November 1996, the Tamagotchi was sold in toy stores and marketed as the original virtual reality pet. It might be described briefly as an egg-shaped handheld Liquid Crystal Display (LCD) video game that comes attached to a chain or bracelet. The key issue underpinning the Tamagotchi was that it could die, and to keep this digital pet alive and happy one had to look after it by answering its needs just as it answers yours. 'This often accompanies a sense of responsibility that makes the bond still stronger. In the case of Tamagotchi, this bond became problematic, since the responsibility was one of keeping the virtual pet alive or letting it die.'[29] Proper care and maintenance of the Tamagotchi was achieved by performing certain parental responsibilities, including feeding, playing games, scolding, medicating and cleaning up after the synthetic pet.

The commercial success of Tamagotchi was huge, and at one point it was believed that just over 3 per cent of the Japanese population owned at least one. 'In [the] case of Tamagotchi, the virtual pet displayed no intelligence. Yet kids and even adults felt seriously engaged in and responsible for the life of the little dot-based creature.'[30] The relationships that resulted from this interaction seemed quite real, so much so that one Japanese child actually committed suicide when their Tamagotchi died.

The manner in which users regard their virtual pets as being of greater emotional value than most other digital objects is of great research interest; insight into this would illuminate the subject–object attachment debate further still by indicating some of the key drivers that motivate users to foster meaningful attachments with electronically mediated objects and experiences. It may be said that the nurturing and caring for another being is a fundamental human need, and the acquisition of pets provides us with a means to gratify this primal urge. Dogs, in particular, have played a central role in the majority of known human societies for nearly 13 millennia; substantial archaeological findings indicate that these animals – not unlike our canine friends today – were an intrinsic element of everyday life. It is not surprising, then, that 12,000 years on in the digital age of virtual reality and artificial intelligence, we find ourselves gazing longingly at Sony's very own puppy AIBO through the window of a high street electronics store.

Although people who engage in relationships with virtual pets such as Tamagotchi will experience a degree of God-like creation, these simulations fail to deliver the psychophysical enormity of the real experience of raising a live pet. The subject is cast within the role of *user* rather than *creator*, as the limited selection of predetermined actions that can be triggered – such as feeding or scolding – are such that the sequence of interactions that does ensue between the subject and the object fail to deliver the nuances of spontaneity, growth and discovery which are so desperately sought. If we as a creative industry are to elevate subject and object interactions beyond *user and used* to *creator and creature*, designers must first increase the intensity and perceptibility of subject–object dependency, enabling products to achieve deeper and more immersive modes of prolonged user engagement. This can be achieved in numerous ways; but if the simulation is not genuine, it will be cast off by the user as gadgetry or a deceiving quirk. The illusion of dependency is therefore insufficient; we must conceive products that actually depend upon users and genuinely need our emotional and physical support in order to survive – facilitating the creation of authentic and meaningful interactive experiences that go beyond the virtual, toward the actual.

Alterity

The authenticity of the experience mediated by the Tamagotchi is enabled largely by its high degree of alterity. Alterity is experienced by users as the feeling that something is both autonomous and is in possession of its own free will; when objects embody this eccentric quality, the relationships forged between subject and object are frequently strong and long lasting. Later developments on the digi-pet theme, such as Sony's PostPet and Dokodemo Issyo, and Sega's Seaman take this phenomenon a step further.

When speaking of alterity, PostPet is of particular interest; co-conceived by artist Kazuhiko Hachiya and Sony Communication Network Corporation in 1998, it provides a fun and game-like email interface in which a small character such as a teddy bear or dog leaves its cosy virtual room on your desktop to deliver email. Sometimes it takes a minute or so to make the delivery before coming back to the room; but once back through the door, another mail can be sent. Unlike the limited feeding requirements of Tamagotchi, consisting of two options of *meal* or *snack*, PostPet may choose from a fine selection of international cuisine; it also gets pudding. In addition, the virtual characters in PostPet have advanced autonomy and occasionally – particularly in times of boredom – develop complete autonomy to become wholly self-governing. 'Differing from Tamagotchi, second-generation pets have their own minds and wills. In PostPet, a virtual pet may make friends with other PostPets by him/herself, might not return home if he/she wants to play with them, or may even start writing e-mail messages without any instruction from the user.'[3] In fact, their autonomy may reach a level where they can actually become quite a nuisance if not stewarded and kept under fairly close supervision.

It is interesting to notice that as the PostPet's level of autonomy increases, the apparent level of dependency it exhibits decreases exponentially as it appears to need and depend upon its user less and less. Although this may enhance the PostPet's eccentric personality, it is questionable as to whether or not it is beneficial to the relationship's longevity; perceptible neediness is, after all, a motivational driver, which could be said to underpin the acquisition of almost all pets, whether virtual or actual.

Cherishability

Back in the physical world we can see how similarly engaging, yet less developed, interactive opportunities await, where a genuine sense of dependency might encourage users to actually care for, nurture and cherish apparently needy objects. The extent to which these somewhat ideological visions may be integrated with the rigid constraints of a commercialized reality must, however be questioned.

In 1996, a design workshop entitled 'Visions of the Future' was held at Philips Corporate Design in Eindhoven. The aim of the workshop was to create new scenarios for a range of products and services for daily life in the year 2005. A number of concepts that emerged from this revolutionary creative workshop possessed enduring qualities remarkably similar to those found in Tamagotchi, PostPet and other dependency-simulating objects. Philips states that:

> Many of the concepts strive to be highly cherishable so that they will be treasured and kept for a long time for their personal symbolic and sentimental

value. Cherishable quality is evident in the Shiva Personal Multi-tasking Personal Assistants, in which the software adapts to fit the user's habits and wishes. It is also found in the little Ludic Robot, whose software learns to recognize its owner's voice and behave with an enduring unpredictability. And clearly … the Emotion Containers, because of their highly personal content, have a high degree of cherishability.'[32]

Through the broad range of examples outlined by Philips, we can see that the term *cherishability* means numerous things, including unpredictable, symbolic, sentimental, adaptive, enduring, personal and dependent, to name but a few. Cherishability is a useful term, a banner beneath which numerous creative product life-extension strategies may fall. Cherishability is a powerful signifier of an object's capacity to be cherished, loved and cared for by whatever means; in this way it is a valuable term for measuring the degree of dependency perceived in a given object. Like empathy, cherishability will, indeed, become an increasingly relevant design consideration in the sustainable marketplace of the future; though before this can happen, greater experimentation is needed regarding the creative methods through which it may be implemented.

Feed-forward and inherent feedback

One method for designing emotionally rich interactions can be drawn from feed-forward and inherent feedback; the term *inherent* is crucial here as it denotes relatedness to the initial input or feed-forward. 'With feed-forward, we mean communication of the purpose of an action … [w]ith inherent feedback we try to strengthen the coupling between the action and the feedback.'[33] Most people are quite comfortable in their understanding of conventional feed-forward and feedback: 'sending back to the user information about what action has actually been done, what result has been accomplished … is a well-known concept in the science of control and information theory.'[34] However, in contrast to conventional feed-forward and feedback methodologies, inherent feedback must reflect the nuances and subtle ambiguities of feed-forward. The car horn is a great example of how not to do this. A car pulls out in front of you, almost causing an accident, and you slam the palm of your hand down on the horn. The horn blares. Pulling up outside your grandmother's flat to take her to bingo, you gently tap the horn with your index finger; the horn blares. In these dissimilar contexts we see two radically different manners of feed-forward. The first is intended to be aggressive and scolding, whereas the second is meant to be more of a chirpy greeting; yet the horn responds the same way in both cases. Although a direct link can be made between the feed-forward – pushing a button – and the feedback – horn blaring – the specific nature of the car horn's feedback is not inherent.

This model of interaction is, indeed, the prevailing commercial norm, and can be found in most product scenarios where buttons, dials and switches are located. In this way the on/off world of commercial goods possesses a banality that somehow transforms the rich wonder of material culture into mundane drudgery. Inherent feedback can help to reduce both the cognitive and emotional gap between subject and object, and may therefore be seen as a primary agent of empathic engagement. 'Engagement is not just something that happens momentarily when we use something. It is also a relationship that has to grow over the years.'[35] When subject–object interactions develop this degree of intuition, the boundaries between flesh and polymer disintegrate to make way for new and provocative modes of material engagement. The black and white world of traditional interaction develops a shade of grey, situated in the fuzzy space between on and off, yes and no.

Fuzzy interaction

Fuzzy interaction reintroduces the wild card element of unpredictability to otherwise traditional interaction scenarios; the overall result is less precise outcomes and richer user experiences. The ideology of fuzzy interactions with objects runs contrary to the prevailing model of popular design, with its focus on idiot-proof user interfaces. However, we should not recoil back from this left-field and less precise model of material engagement simply because it differs from the norm. In many cases, 'imperfections can be endearing and help to create a bond with the user'.[36] It may be, after all, that the brutal discarding of fully functional products is actually catalysed by excessive usability, which leads to the exclusion of error and accidental discoveries; it is quite possible that products designed in this way are simply too predictable, and thus are incapable of holding our interest over any great length of time.

Fuzzy interfaces present users with complex, artful scenarios that must be learned and mastered – a novel departure from the unconsciously simple, spoon-fed manner in which interface design has become accustomed, toward a craft-like engagement in which the skill and mastery of an object must be acquired slowly, over time. Another advantage of fuzzy interactions is that they slow us down, creating what Ezio Manzini refers to as 'islands of slowness'[37] that allow us to think, experience and re-evaluate our assumptions about the way things are in this ever changing world. In recent times, pace has become a measure of progress; today, the pace of life has surpassed the cognitive capabilities of the human brain, forcing us to differentiate between the things we want to think about, and the things we do not. In other words, there is more information out there than we have time to process and therefore we must be selective; we stop thinking about certain things: things that we deem unimportant.

Pace

Many interaction designers are beginning to suspect that as pace increases, experience decreases; this is sometimes referred to as diminishing returns. Although this may not be true in the case of a roller coaster ride or a bungee jump, it does illustrate that the length of the overall interactive engagement should be drawn out in order to maximize the resulting experience. 'Some products allow the user's perception of them to change over time, either by a certain richness of detail or by slowly unfolding, thus displaying more sides of their personalities. They reveal their layers like an onion.'[38] Indeed, the experience provided by a roller coaster is largely speed-oriented, however, without the lengthy queuing period and the slow ascent up to the ride's highest point, the experience would be less rich.

It was discussed earlier in this book that one of the fundamental problems underpinning the consumption and waste of natural resources is that consumers continually evolve, whereas products are frozen in time. Inherent feedback and feed-forward, fuzzy interactions and attention to pace assist in destabilizing this one-way process by encouraging users to re-evaluate the relationship, and subconsciously update their feelings toward a given object. The relationship between subject and object becomes evolutionary, as the subtle exchange of feed-forward and inherent feedback creates the illusion of mutual growth.

Of course, fuzzy interaction is not for everyone, nor is it universally applicable. Not all consumers want to spend ten months learning how to correctly operate their dishwasher, nor would customers be too thrilled if a cash machine issued only what it felt you could afford at that particular time. Nevertheless, alternative modes of interaction serve to remind us that perhaps the streamlining endeavours of modern times have inadvertently stripped the world of all its charm.

The design industries – as a collective and unified whole – have yet to fully connect with the ideologies of sustainability, and perhaps they never will. Born from a lack of genuine interest and belief, a malaise of disinterest and detachment circulates a large percentage of the creative population to render environmental sensibilities a relatively unattractive option. It must be said that not everybody cares about the environmental impacts of design and production, and it is therefore unrealistic to expect each and every single designer to address these issues in an equally committed way. The well-intentioned call of sustainable design is somewhat prescriptive, whereas people – especially design people – do not like being told what to do. It therefore appears clear that imposing the rigid principles of sustainability upon the creative professions in a top-down approach will only serve to stun creativity by threatening the 'blue sky ideology' that creative practitioners hold so very dear:

> … not everyone feels the call to create water-pumps or utility vehicles for local people in Africa, to design wheelchairs and other useful devices or to conceive environmentally friendly products on the basis of detailed lifecycle analyses.[39]

It is vital that we revisit the methods through which we discuss sustainability, and the way in which it is shared, discussed and implemented within creative practice. Essentially, change will not be brought about through telling people what they can and cannot do; the likelihood of change will only occur when alternatives emerge that propose a more attractive solution to the one currently adopted.

Chapter summary

Archaeologists have made numerous findings that suggest the prehistoric origins of material culture. Although the ways in which we manipulate matter today may have developed beyond recognition, our existential and frequently animistic utilization of material artefacts remains unchanged.

. . . .

Many blame the mid 1900s industrial revolution for today's overabundant production, consumption and subsequent environmental decay, stating that such enhanced production capabilities were beyond our control and was like giving a Ferrari to a four-year old.

. . . .

In this oversaturated world of people and things, durable attachments with objects are seldom witnessed; most products deliver a predictable diatribe of information, which quickly transforms wonder into drudgery.

. . . .

Disappointment may be characterized by a real-time imbalance between expectation and reality.

. . . .

The passionate early stages of a subject–object relationship could be described as a honeymoon period. Most emotional attachments are withdrawn once the honeymoon period draws to a close, largely because the evolution that takes place is grossly polarized, occurring exclusively within users.

. . . .

Products make claims that are hard to back up, promising the world to consumers from the safety of the shop window. Although short-term edge may be acquired via this strategy, raising expectations increases the likelihood of disappointment.

. . . .

The emotional instability of humans provides a wild card element to the development of attachments with objects; the development of empathic relationships with objects is powerfully influenced by this characteristic instability.

. . . .

Dependency and neediness often bridge the void between otherwise separate entities, creating relationships founded on the symbiotic exchange of reliance and need. If the simulation is not genuine it will be cast off by the user as gadgetry.

. . . .

Everyday objects that engage the senses invade our lives and literally depend upon our care and attention in order to survive. Designers must aim to increase the intensity and perceptibility of subject–object dependency, enabling products to achieve deeper and more immersive modes of prolonged user engagement.

. . . .

Alterity is experienced by users as the feeling that something is both autonomous and is in possession of its own free will; when objects embody this eccentric quality, the relationships forged between subject and object are frequently strong and long lasting.

. . . .

As an object's level of autonomy increases, the apparent level of dependency decreases exponentially. Although this may enhance an object's eccentricity, it is questionable as to whether or not it is beneficial to a relationship's longevity.

. . . .

Cherishability is a powerful signifier of an object's capacity to be cherished, loved and cared for by whatever means; in this way it is a valuable term for measuring the degree of dependency perceived in a given object.

. . . .

Emotionally rich interactions may be engendered through the incorporation of feed-forward and inherent feedback. Inherent feedback must reflect the subtle ambiguities of feed-forward, enabling the black and white world of traditional interaction to develop a shade of grey, situated somewhere in the fuzzy space between on and off, yes and no.

. . . .

When subject–object interactions develop greater degrees of intuition, the boundaries between flesh and polymer disintegrate to make way for new and provocative modes of material engagement.

. . . .

Fuzzy interfaces present users with complex, artful scenarios that must be learned and mastered – a novel departure from the unconsciously simple, spoon-fed manner in which interface design has become accustomed, toward a craft-like engagement in which the skill and mastery of an object must be acquired slowly, over time.

. . . .

Many interaction designers are beginning to suspect that as pace increases, experience decreases; this is sometimes referred to as diminishing returns.

The experience provided by a roller coaster is pace-oriented; however, without the lengthy queuing period and the slow ascent up to the ride's highest point, the experience would surely be less rich.

. . . .

Alternative modes of interaction serve to remind us that modern streamlining endeavours may have inadvertently stripped the world of all its charm.

A toolbox of ideas

Keep it real: always ensure that objects deliver what they promise. Authenticity plays a crucial role in the nurturing of sustainable subject and object attachments; its absence drives a colossal wedge between subject and object, and what empathy may have been developed prior to this realization promptly disintegrates.

. . . .

Design for dependency: think beyond the conventional master and slave hegemony underpinning contemporary material relations, toward a more synergistic 'consumerscape' in which human and object coexist on a range of physical and emotional levels. In order for this immersive level of engagement to be achieved, the division of responsibility, effort and reward must be shared between subject and object.

. . . .

A mind of its own: give objects the appearance of having a mind of their own, or at least aim to simulate the subtle and random presence of free will. This simulation can be created by engendering a degree of disobedience into products, rendering them less *yes* and *no*, and more *maybe*. A light touch is required here, as excess alterity transforms previously subordinate products into adolescent rogues, which in many cases hit landfill several days later.

. . . .

Inherent feedback: try to initiate interactions of a greater emotional richness and durability by ensuring that feedback is inherent. This is achieved by embodying a distinct relatedness within feedback, with the unique idiosyncrasies of feed-forward, creating several shades of grey between the black and white world of *on* and *off*.

chapter four

authors of experience

User experience

Whether designed that way or not, users invariably have some experience of a manufactured object. Just as we might unwittingly experience a tranquil sunset, the stench of an old wet dog or perhaps a knock at the door in the early hours of the morning, experience may be drawn from all facets of life, and to varying degrees. It is common to hear of user experiences defined in terms of their intensity or power; yet to measure experience in this way is actually counterproductive in a number of instances. Contrary to popular misconception, it is the subtle and more ephemeral user experiences that penetrate the psyche through the slow and steady passing of time. Intense user experiences, such as those gained from igniting a firework, or achieving 0 to 100 kilometres per hour in less than four seconds, for example, are indeed powerful; yet they are fleeting and are seldom revisited by users. In contrast to this, subtle and more ephemeral user experiences, such as those gained from gently refilling a fountain pen with ink, or perhaps re-honing the blade of a sushi knife on a well-worn whet stone, will be revisited time and time again, as with each visit the experience grows and evolves a little further. Therefore, measuring experiences in terms of their apparent intensity is unhelpful as it fails to designate the long-term efficacy – and potential durability – of the experience itself. In addition, it is worth noting that many, perhaps the majority of, user experiences are never even consciously realized; they are perceived only within deeper levels of mental processing, which forge through time meaningful associations with a given product, material or experience. Insignificant as they may at first seem, these subconscious experiences may be the most potent and influential of all. They establish strong and durable connections within users, on both rational and emotional levels.

This point may be exemplified by examining the experience of serving salad from a white ceramic bowl as opposed to one made from reconstituted wood; though both bowls do the same thing – serve salad – the interactive experience they provide differ greatly. The ceramic bowl resonates sharply on contact with the serving utensil, and the zesty hues of the salad are contrasted against the pure white of the ceramic, while the innate perception held by each of us of ceramic as being a pure and precise, and somehow timeless, material embellishes the experience further still. The glazed surface of the ceramic feels cold to the touch, slowly drawing heat from the hand on contact, while reflecting subtle nuances of the salad's colour and shape through the same lustrous, mirror-like surface.

Now take the bowl made from reconstituted wood. Its walls are thicker than that of the ceramic bowl; yet the lower material density also provides a lower overall weight. Due to its non-uniform matrices of wood fragments, the acoustics of this low-density material possess numbness, a softness that engenders the object with a sense of calm. Whether reconstituted or not, wood maintains an ambient temperature that makes it barely discernible to touch. Both the unsystematic undulating surface texture, and myriad patterns formed by the wood particles jostling for position in the moulding process adorn each bowl with a degree of idiosyncrasy and uniqueness. It is fairly common to observe consumers comparing four or five such bowls like-for-like on the shop floor, to find the one with the boldest markings, the richest array of contrasting woody colours, or simply in search of one that stands out in some way. Glorious chance happenings occur during production, which bring their own value to the final piece. Knotty pieces of wood appear in unusual places, or maybe a single oversized wood chip finds its way triumphantly into the mould, elevating the object beyond the anonymous world of mass manufacturing.

These user experiences only lightly scratch the surface of a semiotic and sensorial deconstruction of an object that could conceivably run on for several more pages; we have not even begun to discuss the more fundamentally *designed* elements, such as shape, size and proportion. The point to be made here is that when scrutinized in isolation, these experiences may initially appear somewhat insignificant – perhaps even banal - but when perceived in their collective entirety these subtle, yet potent micro-experiences pull together to construct an aggregate user experience that is both meaningful and often long lasting. With this in mind, it becomes apparent that any object (no matter how menial or commonplace) is capable of eliciting intense arrays of experience within users, and that each design decision (no matter how small) is wholly influential over the way in which users perceive these experiences.

Some, perhaps most, experiences in life cannot be planned and should not be either, such as the experience of falling in love, being overwhelmed by extreme boredom or just simply experiencing the blissful afterglow that follows a fine meal. Life is filled with experiences, all of which may be described as meaningful as they empower us to formulate conceptual frameworks of reference, which serve to rationalize the complex world in which we live. Experience designer Nathan Shedroff claims that:

> While everything, technically, is an experience of some sort, there is something important and special to many experiences that make them worth discussing. In particular, the elements that contribute to superior experiences are knowable and reproducible, which make them designable.[1]

Despite their capricious instability, all experiences can be rationalized, understood and learned from in some way. This process of critical observation is fundamental to design as it provides an endless source of inspiration from which we may gain insight into the way in which we live, and the separate elements that make the process of living both meaningful and experientially rich.

Naughty, naughty

We occasionally see a flip side to user experience, particularly when products are broken, or even more so when they appear functional but actually are not. Stations in the London Underground are great places to observe this kind of user experience in action; the degree of hatred and rage displaced upon the dysfunctional ticket machines is often remarkable and, indeed, very real; the fact that money is involved simply amplifies an already intense situation. Interestingly, a point is reached after the *reject coin* knob has been poked and prodded in every conceivable way when users will begin striking the offending machine, optimistically checking the coin dispenser in the silence separating each barrage of blows. Remarkably, the beating continues, but the money checking stops; then a concluding spurt of punches is thrown as unadulterated punishment to the infuriating contraption before the user finally admits defeat.

Though examples do exist, we seldom witness users affectionately stroking and caressing machines after they perform well; most users, however, are prepared to invest an enormous degree of emotional outlay in dysfunctional objects, such as physically assaulting a broken ticket machine, pressing the buttons irrationally hard on a remote control with duff batteries or clicking a desktop icon an eleventh time because nothing happened the previous ten. These phenomena are demonstrative of the level of influence that manufactured objects have over our day-to-day well-being, while also illustrating that it often is not until something misbehaves that it actually gets noticed. This is, in part, due to the streamlining endeavours of mainstream material culture; interaction has become an unconscious process that we are barely even conscious of until, that is, it misbehaves.

It is worth noting that 'moderate arousal can focus attention and enhance performance, while extreme arousal in the form of tension or anxiety can interfere with performance'.[2] If an object excessively arouses the user, their ability to interact coherently with it deteriorates quickly. The experiences delivered by objects of this nature can be so intense that

Figure 4.1

Dysfunctional products can evoke

potent emotional responses

Source: Photograph by Katherine

Anne Rose © 2005

they begin to conflict with basic usability, transforming interaction into a maddening sequence of failed attempts and misinterpreted cues. A balance is therefore required, which synchronizes optimal degrees of emotional arousal with a consistent measure of usability and performance, enabling the experience of emotional arousal without compromising the fluidity of elementary interaction between the subject and the object.

The attention-grabbing capability of misbehaviour is equally prevalent outside of the made world, a premise that children seem to grasp very early on. What a child craves more than anything is attention, and you do not tend to get much of that when you are playing quietly on the floor with your Lego bricks. Therefore, children will periodically act up, create a fuss and generally misbehave for no apparent reason as a ploy to get noticed, forcing you to acknowledge their presence and, ultimately, give them the attention that they so desperately crave – even if that equates to getting angry and scolding them. In terms of the sustainability of subject–object interaction, a little misbehaviour here and there might actually be a healthy thing; after all, acting directly against the will of the user may well be the clearest and most immediate way of engendering objects with a perceivable degree of autonomy. To misbehave is to be in possession of one's own free will.

Similar in sentiment is the Asian concept of Yin and Yang, in which opposing forces serve to enable the existence of the other. Yang is 'the principle of light, heat, motivation and masculinity in Chinese philosophy that is the counterpart of Yin'.[3] Yin is 'the principle of darkness, negativity, and femininity in Chinese philosophy that is the counterpart of Yang'.[4] It can be seen quite clearly here that the opposing forces of Yin and Yang serve to complement one another, thus creating balance and harmony. If one force takes precedence over the other – as is often experienced in the human body – imbalance occurs and the organism ceases to operate at its optimum levels of efficiency.

Though this ancient Chinese concept may seem obscure to some, the principle of harmony and balance in all things is fairly common to most. We speak of eating and diet in terms of moderation and strive to establish a healthy balance between work, rest and play; we take the rough with the smooth when it comes to the ups and downs of an intimate relationship;

and we are all familiar with the dualistic rhythm of night and day, which are contained within the broader annual cycles of hot and cold weather that come with the changing seasons. These natural principles go out of the window when it comes to the consumption of material objects; it is as though material culture provides a respite from the emotionally draining world outside – a safe place where satisfaction is guaranteed, or your money back.

Some researchers are beginning to suspect that this manner of engagement with our material world is actually counterproductive, being largely responsible for the degree of disappointment and waste so prevalent today. Over the past few decades, consumer culture has lost its balance, grossly polarizing itself toward the happy-ever-after end of the scale: the end where all is sunny, carefree and non-problematic. This is hardly surprising, really. If given the choice of having a stress-free working day full of exhilaration and delight or enduring an agonizing 14-hour serving of desolation and woe, which would you choose? Our expectations of material objects have become so unrealistically high that disappointment is the only inevitable outcome of continued interaction. According to Yin and Yang, material culture has lost its balance and therefore must be swung away from convenience and servitude where it now lies, back toward the labour intensive and temperamental. Once the conceptual balance is restored, it becomes possible to foresee objects with a naughty, cheeky side to their personality: objects that have sudden mood swings; get sick; go through dysfunctional puberties; get bored; or just simply misbehave from time to time. Enhanced degrees of autonomy such as this would certainly provide a more balanced and less dictatorial mode of subject–object engagement, along with a far richer and more diverse array of experiences for the average user.

Designing contemporary genres of emotionally demanding objects that do nothing but provoke and antagonize their users may not be the most effective approach to optimizing product longevity. In some cases, products born of this mindset may actually find themselves being booted out simply for being too high maintenance and, thus, a permanent source of irritation. Most users do not have the time – or the inclination – to train their alarm clock how to tell the time, clean up after their stereo or traipse the dark streets and alleyways in search of the pubescent TV set that stormed out of the house earlier that day. This degree of emotional demand would most likely lead to annoyance on the part of users, and it would be pretty naive to assume that consumers are currently within range of such an intense form of user experience. Nevertheless, a greater degree of emotional resonance and symbolic exchange between users and objects would elevate interaction beyond its current state. This may be easier than it appears as 'wherever objects take part in practices of symbolic exchange, they gain new significance in accordance with the emotions involved in the exchange relation'.[5] Provided that objects are designed with a sufficient degree of openness, they will provide vehicles for this symbolic exchange to occur, and in so doing will incrementally grow and evolve in the eyes of the user as they continually take on new significance and meaning. As the user evolves and grows, so too does the object. 'It is therefore essential to avoid the notion of industrial design objects as static in meaning and appreciate that, like paintings and literary works, their meanings evolve over time.'[6]

More is less

In today's task-oriented and production-centred world, it might be argued that both the ideology and value of user experience has gone somewhat awry. That is not to say that contemporary consumer culture is a barren wasteland devoid of experience but, rather, that interacting within today's technocratic and overly complicated world of goods somehow gestates an overwhelming sense of detachment and dissatisfaction. We have access to more functions, greater choice and far less mechanical failure than that of previous years, yet as users we are still not amused. In terms of user experience, we can see that, in many cases, more is actually giving us less. Yes, products come with an overwhelming profundity of functions onboard today and, yes, we can do far more with our material empires than we could, perhaps, even just a handful of years ago. But what do all these gadgets, gizmos and whatnots offer in the way of qualitative user experience? It must be questioned as to whether the quality, intensity and durability of user experiences have developed with an equal fervour.

The designing and programming of qualitative user experiences is in danger of becoming a secondary bolt-on: a novel set of considerations, waiting patiently in line behind the seemingly *real* design fundamentals, such as ergonomics, material specification, tooling and the like – all of which make major contributions to the overall user experience, but wrongfully claim dominance over less operational and more poetic design methodologies.

It is an increasingly popular assumption amongst the industrial design profession that qualitative user experiences may be engendered by incrementally escalating the utilitarian capabilities of a given object, or by simply bolting on extra functionality. There is nothing new or contemporary about multi-functionality; mobile phones with integral cameras, MP3 players, AM/FM radios and satellite navigation are deeply reminiscent of the Goblin automatic tea-maker of the early 1900s, later known as the Teasmade. Though initially patented in 1934 by its inventors W. H. Brenner Thornton and William Hermann:

> The British Vacuum Cleaner and Engineering Company of London later bought the patent rights and subsequently sold it under the Goblin Teasmade name. The machine retailed at £5 15s 6d and came with a set of two earthenware cups and saucers, a cream jug and a sugar basin.[7]

By the early 1980s, Teasmades came with a built-in night light, multi-band radio, analogue clock and, of course, an alarm with six joyous morning melodies; several variations on this product genre actually came with an integral vase!

Though laced with a nostalgic charm when viewed with hindsight, this manner of creative methodology might best be described as a Swiss Army Knife approach to design: cramming in functions – often at the expense of usability – in an attempt to engender more meaning and offer greater value for money than the competitor's rival product. The Swiss Army Knife approach to design and production is certainly not confined to product design, and has found its way into most aspects of consumer culture. Negotiating the order of a cup of coffee in Starbucks unveils an absolute minefield of choices, options and variations of the hot beverage theme – from your size requirements to your milk ethics – that somehow detracts from the simple desired experience of going out and slurping on a cup of the black stuff. Some would argue that these options are merely symptomatic of a post-modern culture, in which choice – or the illusion of choice – is paramount to the consumer's sense of well-being. It can, however, be overwhelming, and having successfully navigated your way through this beguiling ordering process and found a seat, the taste and quality of the coffee seem somehow unimportant. The point here is that although choice is both a relevant issue and necessary consideration in most areas of production and consumption, it must be managed with care and sensitivity, otherwise it will completely dominate the interaction and, in so doing, detracts from the experience of engaging in a simple, immersive process.

Experience design

As a discipline, *experience design* has only very recently been formally recognized and named; it is a young discipline still very much in its infancy and in this respect may be described as being in a state of continual flux and tentative evolution. It would be ridiculous to assume, however, that material culture was somehow devoid of qualitative user experiences prior to the advent of experience design officialdom, or that the creative industries were somehow oblivious to the experiences that users were, or were not, having prior to the recognition of experience design; indeed, 'the design of experiences isn't any newer than the recognition of experiences'.[8]

Having been defined as an area of potential, the term experience design essentially provides a particular creative context within which practitioners from a broad range of creative disciplines may operate – similar to the way in which giving sustainable design a name has departmentalized it, enabling exploration to continue with a greater depth and specificity, while simultaneously identifying it as a relevant issue to the profession as a whole. Many creative practitioners are beginning to question the efficacy of this approach since departmentalizing frequently serves to exclude as much as it includes, giving rise to a them-and-us culture in which separatist design sects emerge that exist in apparent isolation from one another. This is a highly disadvantageous destiny for designers to pursue as it inhibits the cross-pollination of creative disciplines, which in a number of scenarios provides the very life blood of innovation.

Contrary to popular belief, experience design does not simply confine itself to the fields of digital media and human–computer interaction (HCI). 'Experience design is an emerging paradigm, a call for inclusion: it calls for an integrative practice of design that can benefit all designers.'[9] Certainly, the work of experience designers has tended to centre itself within the digital sphere and continues to do so to this day; however, the discipline's potential stretches far beyond the design of online media:

> Designers who work in the physical world of themed products and environments have a vastly more developed theoretical base they can call on than do designers who work in the online world. While the latter have recently gotten the most ink, a lot more money and labour goes into the design of tangible objects and places intended to engender experiences. Designers in the physical world also have developed rigorous project-management and client-service skills, as well as a heightened ability to work with cross-disciplinary teams. Comparable skills and methods are not prolific among online designers.[10]

User experience has always been an important design consideration, yet, regrettably, a consideration rarely applied to mundane everyday genres of objects; this is most likely why they are still described as being mundane and everyday. A website, for example, will receive a great deal of attention from experience designers, whereas objects such as wash basins, toilet seats and ironing boards – which cater for equally commonplace user experiences – may receive little or no consideration at all in terms of user experience.

Experience design and the creative principles that it encompasses may be applied to almost any designable scenario, whether a computer game, travelling exhibition, household appliance, or a 50-storey building for that matter. The key point is that where there is potential for experience, so, too, is there a potential for experience design:

> The most important concept to grasp is that all experiences are important and that we can learn from them, whether they are traditional, physical, offline experiences or whether they are digital, online or other technological experiences.[11]

In today's increasingly experience-oriented marketplace, it is easy to see how this new and experimental design discipline has a key role to play. The very existence of it provides a signpost to the future direction that design is facing as a collective amalgamation of subdisciplines.

As an area of creative practice, experience design might best be described as a synthesis of contemporary design disciplines that, when interlaced, facilitate the generation of creative solutions to a broad range of modern-day problems. One of the key strengths of this new branch of design lies in its interdisciplinary nature. By cross-pollinating previously isolated disciplines, experience design manages to pioneer alternative and revealing possibilities for the future. According to the American Institute of Graphic Arts (AIGA), experience design is 'a different approach to design that has wider boundaries than traditional design and that strives for creating experiences beyond just products or services'.[12] Although constructed on a foundation of traditional design principles, experience design transcends them, and in so doing is empowered to take a more holistic approach to the creation of product life cycles, attending not only to the creation of durable, mass-manufactured objects and experiences, but also in the engendering of perceivably individualistic user experiences. AIGA have found that this level of subject–object intimacy may be further engendered by 'creating a relationship with individuals, not targeting a mass market'.[13] The offerings of experience design may leave the factory floor in the tens of thousands; however, the experiences that users glean from them are both unique and, quite notably, idiosyncratic.

Experience design puts forward a more empathic approach than that of conventional design by proposing emergent consumer futures that facilitate the satisfaction of commercial, societal and individual needs. It is a qualitative process, which encompasses the planning, research, conceptualization, design and development of a vast array of user-centric objects and experiences. It is unfortunate that:

> ... the intense time and project pressures faced by designers in all disciplines, together with a parochialism or provincialism that is disturbingly constant among designers, prevents interdisciplinary conversations. Web designers are too busy to talk to architects, who are too busy to talk to graphic designers, who are too busy to talk to automotive designers and so on.[14]

A more ecumenical approach would encourage greater diversity and pluralism within the creative industry, smashing down the walls of distinction that currently sequester design disciplines from one another to unveil a wider and more collaborative creative culture.

The creative methodologies utilized by experience designers explore diverse and frequently abstract territories that are not ordinarily associated with commercial design practice and processes. For example, theatre, dance and performance may be used as tools to assist communication with clients, enabling ideas and concepts to be mediated through dramatic, yet readily cognizable, means. Storytelling also plays a large part in the mediation of complex narratives and may be deployed by experience designers and information architects as a means of organizing and rationalizing complex assemblages of data. In this way, it can be seen that the exploratory, experimental nature of experience design is actually one of its greatest strengths; through resisting categorization within a predefined design genre, a seemingly limitless world of possibility becomes immediately accessible to all who follow its principles. Thus, online designers find themselves developing navigational signage solutions for publicly funded buildings, while interior designers might work on the internal arrangement of radical automotive concepts. Interdisciplinary cross-collaboration of this kind is becoming ever more prolific, and provides testimony to the emergent notion that the experience in itself is becoming as important, if not more important, than the actual medium that delivers it.

In commercial terms, user experience could be defined as 'the perception resulting from the experiences a person has with a company, its products and its services at every point where that company touches their lives'.[15] This indicates that the experience delivered by a product may not be fully distinguished from that of the brand, and its own complex array of values and associations – a phenomena which adds yet another beguiling layer of complexity to the process of planning (or authoring) qualitative user experiences. For example, the experience of drinking Coke's new line of bottled water is tainted by our overall associations with the brand; similarly, a Caesar salad from McDonald's seems somehow less nutritious than one bought from the family-run deli next door.

When examined in depth, experience design seems to put forward a fairly complex assemblage of interlinked issues and principles; yet through engagement and exploration, this complexity becomes less apparent as new realities emerge through participation and experimentation, which transcend the restrictive rationality of rules and principles.

Experience and emotion

In today's restless world of unceasing technological miniaturization, the need for objects capable of purveying potent emotional resonance is greater than ever. This is not to say that product miniaturization is necessarily commensurate with experience decline; rather, as the objects we deploy to designate our particular being reduce in size, their metaphysical properties must expand in order to compensate for the lack of physical presence:

> Issues of emotion, affective response and inclusive human concerns are exceedingly important in design. As people become more sensitive to dimensions of products that go beyond traditional aspects of usability, the need to understand and create emotional and aesthetic resonance between people and products increases.[16]

This notion of co-sustainability between both the physical and metaphysical attributes of objects is particularly interesting in the current digital age; the enormity of this concept, however, has yet to be realized by the industry as a whole, which seems to be strangely preoccupied with maintaining currency with the technological state of the art. In migrating toward the virtual, we become in danger of subscribing to an experience-impoverished future: an immaterial world of trite engagements with anonymous objects, devoid of qualitative user experiences. It is imperative that designers identify with this notion by pushing creative practice beyond the size-oriented and speed-focused present to explore the deeper metaphysical dimensions of objects and experiences.

The role of emotion in design is of mounting importance. Having established itself as a fundamental branch of design discourse within the latter part of the 20th century, emotion continues to adopt an ever more prevalent position within contemporary design debate today. Of course, emotion has always played an elementary function in all forms of design and creation, both from the creator's perspective and also from that of the end user. Since the beginning, the process of designing has been firmly rooted within emotional terms and taxonomies; the language that designers deploy to describe objects frequently ventures into emotional accounts of how they make us feel, what they remind us of, or what persona the objects seem to portray. Users will powerfully associate emotional characteristics with the slightest and most subtle of visual cues; colours play a large part in emotional attribution, with a range of hot pinks being described in terms ranging from sullen and melancholy to joyous and even lustful, while deep purples are often perceived as decadent and bourgeois. Cars are commonly said to have happy or sad faces based solely on the configuration of headlamps and radiator grills, whereas a house may be described as having a friendly feel, a welcoming ambience or perhaps even a calm and restful aura.

A considerable amount of information and knowledge has been generated on the subject of emotion, experience and the emotional values attributed to mass-manufactured objects. Despite the fact that emotions play a part in almost all facets of life, they are to this day very much shrouded in mystery. Furthermore, it must be questioned as to whether the contribution made by this discourse is of any worth. 'Has this recent emphasis on emotions in design generated a critical insight? Can we foresee – or should we already see – its positive as well as negative outcomes in individual as well as social life?'[17]

It may not be possible to establish a semantic connection between emotions and the very notion of experience or, perhaps, to pin human emotions down within a succinctly unified theory. Dr Gerald Cupchik – professor of psychology at the University of Toronto – integrates emotion with aesthetics; the span of his research is far reaching and includes some fascinating insights on emotional response and industrial design. He claims that:

> Emotional processes involved in generating and using industrial design objects have only begun to be explicated. They begin with an initial impression of the object, continue through actual experiences utilizing it, and culminate with degrees of emotional attachment to it.[18]

He further claims that the formula 'cognitive meaning + arousal = emotion merges the analytical approach of British empiricism with the mechanistic principles of behaviourism'.[19] This formula is helpful as it begins to unpack the problem by deconstructing the genesis of emotion down into three elementary stages in a process. His theory indicates that a meaningful association must first be perceived within an object before users may experience any arousal and subsequent emotion. Or, to put it another way, cognitive meaning provides the essential foundation upon which arousal and emotion are constructed.

Donald Norman, behavioural scientist and promoter of human-centred products and services, contrasts this view, claiming that 'emotions are inseparable from and a necessary part of cognition. Everything we do, everything we think is tinged with emotion, much of it subconscious.'[20] He further develops the theory that design – and the way in which we interact with and process designed objects – may be split into three distinct parts consisting of a *visceral*, a *behavioural* and, finally, a *reflective* element. Norman calls upon his three favourite teapots to illustrate the point:

> *Visceral* design concerns itself with appearances. Here is where the Nanna teapot excels – I so enjoy its appearance, especially when filled with the amber hues of tea, lit from beneath by the flame of its warming candle. *Behavioural* design has to do with the pleasure and effectiveness of use. Here both the tilting teapot and my little metal ball are winners. Finally, *reflective* design considers the rationalization and intellectualization of a product. Can I tell a story about it? Does it appeal to my self image, to my pride?'[21]

These three stages are indeed useful, while also being fairly comprehensive both as independent stages in a cognitive process, and as a conceptual whole.

A cross-examination of the theories put forward by both Cupchik and Norman would be somewhat counterproductive, as both assist in generating equally valuable insight to the problem of understanding the psychological processes that take place during subject–object interaction. The fact that they simultaneously contradict and support one another is indicative of the current level of understanding; recognizing the particular manner in which we respond emotionally to the made world is a work in progress. Despite this, it is already tacit to most creative practitioners that emotions do play a key role in engendering resonant experiences within users, and this awareness in itself may well be enough. However, the simple fact that we have a name for each emotion does not mean that we understand them; just as we have a name for the universe or, perhaps, the ancient Chinese system the *I-Ching*, they are both very much beguiling and far from understood. In instances such as these, names facilitate the communication of general concepts; terms used to define emotions such as love, jealousy and melancholia also act in such a way to provide general terms of reference to which each of us may have our own particular interpretation that is based primarily on our accumulated experiences. Though we have names for each emotion that enable us to differentiate between them on a semantic level, emotions do not actually exist in isolation; 'emotions are compounded phenomena involving expressive, behavioural, experiential and physiological facets'.[22] In this way it can be seen that emotions are far more complex than they first appear. They are inexplicably intertwined, making their origins practically indistinguishable.

Countless theories abound that attempt to rationalize human emotions by mapping them onto various conceptual frameworks and within numerous theoretical models – whether an incendiary statement from the edgy world of contemporary art, philosophical musings from the likes of Sartre and Plato or perhaps academic rationale from the most advanced of clinical psychologists. An adequate explanation of human emotion has yet to reveal itself. This fact should not deter us, as it is within the peculiarity, the randomness and the idiosyncrasies of human emotion that the real design potential lurks. Emotional responses make up the very foundations of individuality; they are what distinguish us from others. Through choice, simulation and association, products provide triggers for this vital sociological process to occur. If anything, a clear and unified theory that explains the origin, purpose and rationality of emotion would only serve to detract from the intuitive potency of design, effectively stripping another layer of charm from this over-explained world. The Design and Emotion Society claims that:

The concept of experience, where the subject and object meet and merge with one another, is a key issue in designing emotionally meaningful products.

This is because experience is a space in which all faculties, especially emotions, are activated.[23]

In addition, a given emotional response to an object will be largely dictated by the prior experiences of the onlooker. It follows, therefore, that emotions must also exist within a wider cultural context since the way we interact with and respond to the world is largely conditioned by our prior experiences. 'In each culture there are symbols that elicit favourable emotions shared by all members.'[24]

It is clear that although a designer can certainly elicit within users an emotional response to a given object, the explicit nature of the response is beyond the designer's control; the unique assemblage of past experiences that is particular to each user, their cultural background and life journey determine this:

> People can differentially attend to the sensory qualities of the design object and attach diverse personal meanings onto it because they see it used in various contexts. Their reactive emotions will therefore reflect personal associations and meanings which are projected onto the object.[25]

This might actually be one of the most crucial and relevant premises to grasp when designing experientially rich interactions between people and things, as these idiosyncrasies elicit powerful sensations of individuality and uniqueness within users; therefore, no two people will perceive the same object in exactly the same way:

> Personal/symbolic meanings relate to self-concept and dynamic processes affecting both a person's motivation for engaging an industrial design object and also how it is seen. These motivations can lead a person to project supplementary meanings onto industrial objects which may not be directly related to their functions or appearances.[26]

As mentioned earlier, the way in which a user will perceive an object is largely influenced by the accumulative nature of their prior experiences; it follows therefore that:

Personal experiences and emotional meanings complete the image of the object whose appearance and functions are but initial cues as to their broader meaning. The more an individual consciously or unconsciously relates to the sensory/aesthetic, cognitive/behavioural, and personal/symbolic qualities of an object, the more profound will be the attachment.[27]

The designer's role could simply be to provide material artefacts that provoke some kind of emotional response from the user – whatever that may be – as users will ultimately project their own personality onto the object just as long as it continues to stimulate a response. The issue now becomes the sustainability, or life cycle, of that crucial emotional response.

In most instances, users begin to accumulate emotional histories with objects from the moment of purchase; it could also be argued that in many cases this accumulative process initiates itself prior to purchase, as the most primitive connections between subject and object are often forged through shop windows, television commercials or, perhaps, from the pages of catalogues and magazines where the product was first initially eyed. Most design researchers agree that it is desirable to create products that sustain their emotional content throughout the entire span of their physical life, and in simple terms this premise is accurate. However, emotional presence alone is insufficient; evolution and growth must also be present if the relationship between subject and object is to develop intimacy through the passing of time. Furthermore, the accumulation of emotional history is dependent upon this kind of growth, as without it objects quickly stagnate. 'It is one thing to design products that elicit certain emotions; it is another matter to maintain those emotions that have been generated.'[28] Although the overall hypothesis of this quote is, indeed, helpful in highlighting an issue that is commonly overlooked by designers, the term *maintain* may not actually be so helpful. To maintain is 'to make a situation or course of action continue in the same way as before'.[29] This, of course, is not what is needed if we are to close the gap between subject and object; instead, the term *develop* may be more helpful as what is actually needed is a steady evolutionary growth that occurs both in sync and in reaction to the user, and absolutely not to keep things the same as they were before:

> When particular stimulus properties modulate simple feelings of pleasure
> or arousal, the basic principles of behaviourism readily apply. For example,
> repeated exposure to a stimulus will reduce its potency for eliciting pleasure or
> arousal through the principle of habituation.[30]

In failing to evolve, the intensity and meaning of a given stimulus crumbles
away simply through familiarity and repetition. Overplaying your favourite
CD provides a similar experience; the once soul-defining beauty of a
particular track slowly transforms through repetition into a nauseating
taunt, so sickeningly familiar that it almost becomes painful to hear. Some
vinyl aficionados have to hold themselves back, refraining from playing their
favourite 12-inch through sheer avoidance of the inevitable fate that awaits
an overplayed and over-familiarized track.

Experience, and the stimulation that it provides, is not simply an
inconsequential facet of entertainment or some whimsical means through
which to pass the time; it incorporates rich elements of newness, novelty
and uncertainty within the discursive engagement between subject and
object. These new elements are vital ingredients of sustained interaction
as they help to infuse that essential measure of connectedness between
user and product, sustaining attention spans and relieving users from
the monotony of an otherwise stimulus-impoverished engagement. The
particular nature of the stimulus is also of great importance: 'novelty in a
stimulus can generally increase arousal, while uncertainty (in a detective
novel or suspense film) might alleviate a state of boredom or low arousal'.[31]
The way in which the stimulus is experienced may, therefore, be controlled
to some degree and, ultimately, be deployed to alleviate boredom and
under-stimulation, or alternatively to cultivate an edgy state of uncertainty
and doubt.

Immersive experience

In an experiential context, to be immersed is 'to become completely
occupied with something, giving all your time, energy or concentration to
it'.[32] As a pebble plunged into a glass of water, user consciousness becomes
swamped in the all-encompassing act of engagement to a level where
nothing else exists: a kind of meditative state where the conceptual barriers

separating flesh from polymer dissolve away to create oneness between the subject and the object. Popular examples of this kind of immersive experience include virtual reality (VR), juggling, watching a thriller or perhaps having a heated argument. When interacting with the day-to-day offerings of conventional design, however, users seldom experience this degree of immersion. Few can testify to having ever experienced oneness with their potato peeler, and you may be hard pushed to find a consumer who has gelled on a holistic and metaphysical level with their bath taps. That said, degrees of immersion are prevalent in most – if not all – forms of subject–object engagement, and on some level, even the most banal and meaningless tools are capable of inducing some measure of immersive experience, brought about quite simply by enabling users to calmly engage in the process of using the object until conscious influence partially recedes – enabling the conceptual unification of tool and hand. Similarly, when the experience of using and interacting with the product becomes greater than the physical product itself, conscious recognition of the product drops back to make way for full cognition of the experience.

Immersive experiences are both intense and all encompassing. The meaningful associations that users project upon objects capable of delivering such experiences possess a similar potency, and frequently catalyse robust emotional connections between subject and object. It therefore follows that immersive experiences play a role in forging strong attachments between subject and object, and that these experiences possess a far greater validity than simply to entertain, or sustain, attention span. Design culture columnist Wendy Richmond supports the value of these experiences by stating that 'a primary ambition of a designer is to deeply engage his or her audience'.[33] Richmond continues by further claiming that 'the best interactive experiences are ones that are immersive, that is, where you are deeply involved in the subject matter.'[34]

It is often not until an object is interacted with – and used – that it is fully understood. To quote the words of Confucius: *I hear and I forget. I see and I remember. I do and I understand.* Though it may be possible for users to learn about an object via some literary means, such as an instruction manual, or perhaps through word of mouth as is often the case, it is only really through immersion that objects become known and, thus, wholly understood. This point is of particular prevalence in the case of objects with complete or partially screen-based user interfaces, such as mobile phones, Personal Digital Assistants (PDAs) and computers, which must be engaged with on intuitive levels before any qualitative understanding may be achieved. In addition, immersion is a contemplative process that requires a more prolonged and temporally drawn out mode of interaction; due to the increasing speed of interaction today, this is becoming harder to achieve as engagements with objects become ever more fleeting.

The pace at which we live today is excessive, to put it mildly. As people rush frenetically from place to place, confusing activity with accomplishment, it is vital that we as designers remain critical of this behaviour and – more importantly – of its actual efficacy. Slowing down the feverish pace of interaction between people and things must not be revered as a commercially debilitating act or simply a nostalgic hark back to days of yore, when life apparently ran at a far more civilized pace. To propose slower modes of material engagement is to equally propose a deeper and potentially richer experiential landscape of user experiences in everyday life. In the instance of interacting with objects, speed is particularly anti-evolutionary. As in the case of any interactive process, excess speed can be highly counterproductive since it forces gross generalizations to be hurriedly made, while also allowing those engaged in the said process to superficially overlook a great deal. By destabilizing both the fluidity and pace of subject–object interaction, users are empowered with the right to stop, think and contemplate what they are doing and, ultimately, why they are doing it. The way would then be paved for new and provocative genres of objects whose layers of meaning may be peeled back at differing rates of fruition, enriching the qualitative substance of the user experiences that we as design entrepreneurs essentially aim to deliver.

Technology is changing; but then it always has been as transience is fundamental to its nature. One notable change that is beginning to show itself is that of ambient technologies, which are said to deliver experiences that are both immersive and smart. Domestic electronics giant Philips believes that 'in the year 2020, people will relate to electronics in more natural and comfortable ways as we do now'.[35] This is, of course, a fairly safe assumption, though one that is, nonetheless, valid as it clearly illustrates the direction we collectively face as an industry: toward greater comfort facilitated by less interaction. This vision may strike you as reminiscent of the countless depictions of the future that were promised during the 1950s, 1960s and 1970s. Yet, if you take a quick glance around, you will notice that we are not wearing silver foil bodysuits or eating a three-course meal from a single red pill, nor are you likely to have spent any quality vacation time on the moon in recent months. Therefore, visions of the future should be approached with slight caution, as they are seldom realized in their entirety; the value of these visions lies in their ability to illustrate both the direction and orientation of recent culture – lighting the way ahead, as it is currently understood within today's terms of reference.

For many, future casts simply depict utopian and idealized futures of optimized control, convenience and efficiency; and there is, of course, nothing wrong with this. However, other views are very much needed that provide alternatives to the capitalist model of master and slave, and hegemonic material engagements. When discussing the designing of immersive user experiences, Valerie Casey – creative director of San Francisco's Frog Design – states that conventional usability rules do not, and should not, always apply. 'Current [usability] practice is over-rationalized and focuses too deeply on task analysis and not enough on empathy.'[36] As discussed earlier, functionality is not necessarily commensurate with qualitative user experiences and may, in fact, serve to the contrary.

In a technologically streamlined world, the dominant version of reality comes with the majority of problems already solved; all too frequently, we hear of technological innovation being discussed in terms of its ability to remove the decision-making process from humans, while the prevailing design perception of effective user interaction is similarly one of consumers promptly doing exactly what they are told without confusion or debate. Although helpful in certain cases, this model of prosaic interaction numbs the psyche and diminishes the intensity and consequent sustainability of user experiences.

The Philips vision of 'Ambient Intelligence' is 'people living easily in digital environments in which the electronics are sensitive to people's needs, personalized to their requirements, anticipatory of their behaviour and responsive to their presence'.[37] It is also clearly stated by Philips that 'one of the key aspects of Philips's Ambient Intelligence vision is to enrich the user experience'.[38] These are bold goals to set out and goals that, if achieved, would undoubtedly make a valuable contribution to the experiential fabric of daily life. However, we must remain mindful that if users become too comfortable with electronics and are allowed to live too easily within their domestic digital environments, there may, in fact, be very little experience left to enrich.

Conventional design has a propensity for dehumanizing technology, opting to deal with it in terms of minimalist nothingness characterized by an almost supernatural lack of physical presence. This mindset is reinforced further still by the endeavours of miniaturization, where our technological genius as a species may be summed up by the degree of smallness one is able to achieve in a given product scenario. Power and speed will always be of prime importance to technological innovation; it seems that where ambient technologies are concerned, size is the key performance indicator. In technological terms, the physicality of material culture is declining exponentially with the user experiences that it endeavours to deliver. It appears that 'mainstream technological development is heading for a world in which you wander around detached and godly without the need to be in touch with matter anymore'.[39] Indeed, immateriality presents a number of new and interesting experiential possibilities for users, while also hinting at a possible reduction in the consumption and waste of materials due to a reduction in product mass. For these simple reasons alone, miniaturization is a creative destiny worthy of pursuit, though it must also be argued that a greater diversity in technological mediation is required.

Interacting within today's technocratic and anonymous assemblage of miniature digital artefacts can leave one cold. Objects have become excessively subservient, and 'the computational and communicative devices that now assist almost every transaction in our daily lives are designed as dull and servile boxes that respond to our commands in a state of neutrality; stress and techno-phobia are the result'.[40] It must be questioned as to whether this level of material autonomy is actually healthy – like having a house full of domestic servants essentially strips the experience away from daily life by leaving us as users with nothing to do. At this point, technology's role becomes nothing more than a passive, reassuring hum in the background, subordinately informing us that all is well, and that your anonymous assemblage of digital *objets d'art* are doing exactly what they should be and are able to function quite happily without outside help. Hey user, we don't need you anymore; but thanks for the offer.

Chapter summary

To measure experiences in terms of their intensity or power is counterproductive. It is the subtle and more ephemeral user experiences that penetrate the psyche through the slow passage of time.
. . . .
Most user experiences are never consciously realized; they are perceived only within deeper levels of processing.
. . . .
Seldom do we witness users affectionately stroking and caressing machines after they perform well; it often is not until something misbehaves that it actually gets noticed.
. . . .
Whether planned that way or not, users will have some degree of experience from interacting with practically any object. The crucial thing is to both sustain and evolve that experience so that it is revisited and frequently re-evaluated by the captivated user.
. . . .
If an object excessively arouses the user, their ability to interact coherently with it deteriorates quickly.
. . . .
A little misbehaviour here and there is a healthy thing; acting directly against the user's will engenders a high degree of autonomy.
. . . .
Emotionally demanding objects that do nothing but provoke and antagonize their users may not live long. They are too high maintenance and, thus, a permanent source of irritation.
. . . .
The Swiss Army Knife approach to design crams in functions often at the expense of usability in an attempt to engender meaning.
. . . .
Qualitative user experiences are not engendered by incrementally escalating the utilitarian capabilities of a given object or by simply by bolting on extra functionality.
. . . .

The work of experience designers has tended to centre itself within the digital sphere; however, the discipline's potential stretches far beyond the design of online media.

· ⁝ · · · · · · · · · ·

User experience has always been a design consideration; yet it is a consideration rarely applied to mundane everyday genres of objects.

· ·

In today's restless world of unceasing technological miniaturization, the need for objects capable of purveying potent experiential and emotional resonance is greater than ever.

· ·

The role of emotion established itself as a branch of design discourse within the latter part of the 20th century, adopting an ever more prevalent position within contemporary design debate today.

· ·

It may not be possible to establish a semantic connection between emotions and the very notion of experience or, perhaps, to pin human emotions down within a succinctly unified theory.

· ·

It is already tacit to most creative practitioners that emotions play a key role in engendering resonant user experiences; this awareness in itself may actually be enough.

· ·

That we have a name for each emotion does not mean we understand them. We have names for the universe and the ancient Chinese system the *I-Ching*; yet both are far from understood.

· ·

Emotional responses provide the foundations of individuality: they are what distinguish us from others. Products provide triggers for this vital sociological process to occur.

· ·

Although designers can elicit emotional responses, the explicit nature of the response is beyond control. The unique assemblage of past experiences particular to each user determines this.

· ·

Designers need only provoke an emotional response – whatever that may be – as users will ultimately project their personality onto the object just as long as it continues to stimulate that vital response.

· ·

Immersive experiences are all encompassing, provoking meaningful associations that frequently catalyse robust emotional connections between subject and object.
. . . .
In failing to evolve, the intensity and meaning of a given stimulus crumbles away simply through familiarity and repetition.

A toolbox of ideas

Strike a balance: emotionally demanding objects that do nothing but provoke and antagonize their users may not live long; they are too high maintenance and, thus, a permanent source of irritation. Always aim to establish equilibrium between optimal degrees of emotional arousal, with a consistent measure of usability and performance. This will facilitate the smooth delivery of rich and emotionally charged experiences without compromising the behavioural fluidity of elementary subject–object interaction.
. . . .
Provoke a response: design objects that provoke some kind of emotional response from the user. The way in which we each respond emotionally to given stimuli is what both separates and defines us as unique individuals; therefore, creating objects and experiences that provoke a distinct and clear emotional response – whatever the response may be – will engender the felt sense of individuality, self-definition and the affirmation of identity within users.
. . . .
Designers also consume: when attempting to design for and anticipate an emotional response, start by evaluating your own responses to things and consider how you might perceive a given experience. As designers we are fortunate to have experience as both creators and end users; it is crucial that this simple fact is never forgotten as intuitive insight frequently provides the most potent creative tool.
. . . .
Create meaning: a meaningful association must first be perceived within an object before users may experience any arousal and subsequent emotion. Easily cognizable meanings provide the essential foundation upon which arousal and emotion are constructed. Therefore, it is helpful to consider how an object will be perceived by the user and what meanings may be associated with that initial perception.

chapter
five
sustaining
narrative

A metaphysical rendering of newness

Against the commercial backdrop of newer, shinier things, the implementation of desirable ageing strategies appears impromptu. Surely the modern-day societal preoccupation to maintain glossy scratch-free worlds leaves no room for alternative, less transient modes of existence? The current model of industrialism has practically built itself around this ideal, delivering endless streams of faster, lighter, smarter and newer things – greasing the wheels of capitalism by stimulating the consumer demand for more, while maintaining the illusion of progress through constant, yet superficial, innovation for its own sake.

Beneath the silken skin of this mass-manufactured illusion, harsh contradictions dwell regarding the explicit nature of the newness that consumers actually desire. These are inconsistencies that, if addressed, might project us beyond this physical world of glossy surfaces and smooth lines toward a metaphysical interpretation of newness based on the evolution of user experiences, sensations and emotions as encountered through complex interactions with objects – enabling users to sculpt rich and individually crafted narratives that map subject–object relationships as they evolve over time.

Durable narrative experience

Objects capable of delivering durable narrative experiences already pollute the mainstream, and with surprising diversity. These include products that are meticulously repaired and upgraded, objects that are kept for vast periods of time, sometimes spanning generations, and other material possessions that are cherished, nurtured and even loved by users. 'It is no revelation that consumers possess objects to which they are strongly and weakly attached.'[1] However, the existence of emotionally durable artefacts has – thus far – remained cautiously quarantined within low-tech product genres as though their proliferation might slow down consumption of the all-important digital product.

Houseplants provide a pertinent example of a low-tech narrative experience. Once severed from the Earth and placed in a pot, they can either flourish or flag depending upon the degree of care invested in them. In return for water, sunlight and careful situation away from draughts, the plant will give you lush green feedback that your efforts have been recognized. Should the plant fail to do this – and perhaps start dying – most users will modify their approach and invest further effort to assist recovery. Sophisticated physical experiences such as houseplants somehow transcend the day-to-day trivia of material life and thus hold a sacred place in the hearts and minds of users. This affords them a more elevated status than the often prosaic offspring of the mass-manufactured world.

Perhaps through their patient yet tangible forms of feedback, owners are able to perceive a non-programmed response that renders the plant conscious on some level. Consciousness is frequently interpreted by consumer as a sense that something has autonomy – a set of intentions based purely around one's own particular existence – or something that seems to be in possession of its own free will or alterity. 'Alterity relations [are] the dimension of an interaction in which the object of one's intention is perceived in terms of otherness. This particularly elusive concept could be described as the felt sensation of the interaction with an autonomous or intelligent object, animal or individual.'[2]

Just noticeable difference

Objects that evolve slowly over time build up layers of narrative by reflecting traces of the user's invested care and attention. When describing the psychophysics of perceivable change – psychophysics is the branch of experimental psychology concerned with human sensation and perception – cognitive scientist Donald A. Norman speaks of 'just noticeable difference' (JND).[3] JNDs define the necessary amount that something must be altered in order for the difference to be noticeable and perceivable. The principle of JND is illustrated clearly in 'boiled frog syndrome'.[4] The principle here is that if you take a frog and drop it into boiling water, the shock will certainly kill the frog instantly. However, if you were to place the frog in a pan of cold water and gently increase the heat, the frog will actually adapt to quite high temperatures before it notices that it is too hot. 'The frog has a fatal flaw',[5] explains psychologist Robert Ornstein. Having no evolutionary experience with boiling water, 'he is unable to perceive it as dangerous'.[6] Throughout their biological evolution, frogs have lived in a medium that does not vary greatly in temperature, so they have not needed to develop sophisticated thermal detectors in their skin. The frog in the pot is unaware of the threat and simply sits complacently until he boils.

Incremental growth, as is found in both houseplants and boiled water advances in micro-steps that only begin to show their presence through the passing of time. A plant's growth rate is not immediately perceivable in real time; yet, on returning home from a two-week holiday the noticeable growth can be startling. The amorphous transience found in plants demands a degree of patience that for some strange reason is readily accepted by consumers and is found rewarding by most, an emotional commitment so rarely encountered in the made world.

Creator and creature

In the slick and streamlined world of mass-manufactured goods, a handful of transient storytellers still roam unchecked. Denim jeans have successfully delivered narrative experiences to countless users for decades and are surely here to stay:

> You have a close relationship with your jeans. Your jeans are a second skin, faded and shaped and ripped and bulged by your experiences. They are lived in. After a party they smell like a party. They are a familiar old friend, a repository of memories, a comfort blanket.[7]

Where the phrase *denim jeans* originated, no one is quite sure. Although synonymous with Americana, the textile denim is believed to have originated in France some time during the 17th century. 'Most reference books say that denim is an English corruption of the French phrase *serge de Nimes*, a serge fabric from the town of Nimes in France.'[8] This robust textile was imported *en masse* by Levis Strauss in the US in order to clothe manual labourers during the great San Francisco Gold Rush of the mid 1800s. Its commercial growth began when:

> Levi Strauss and a Nevada tailor joined forces to patent an idea the tailor had for putting rivets on [the] stress points of [a] workman's waist-high overalls commonly known as jeans. Levi Strauss chose to use the stronger denim fabric and cotton duck, putting his own name on the product. Later the duck fabric was dropped as consumers found denim more comfortable, particularly after washing creating the faded bloom on the indigo blue dyeing that we all love.[9]

The high street fashion dominance of these garments was not truly established until the 1950s, however, after American heroes such as Brando, Dean and Presley wore them; teenagers of the era eagerly emulated their idols, and the die was well and truly cast.

Interestingly, a textile that was commonly known as *jean* was prevalent even before this time, so called because it originated in Genoa, Italy:

> It was apparently quite popular and imported into England in large quantities during the 16th century. By the end of this period, jean was being produced in Lancashire. By the 18th century, jean cloth was made completely of cotton and used to make men's clothing, valued especially for its property of durability even after many washings.[10]

Today, denim jeans are known for their durability, strength and unique ability to accumulate character through use. When you next wear jeans, remember that 'these pants are a direct descendant of the original pair made in 1873. And it was two visionary immigrants, Levi Strauss and Jacob Davis, who turned denim, thread and a little metal into the most popular clothing product in the world – blue jeans.'[11]

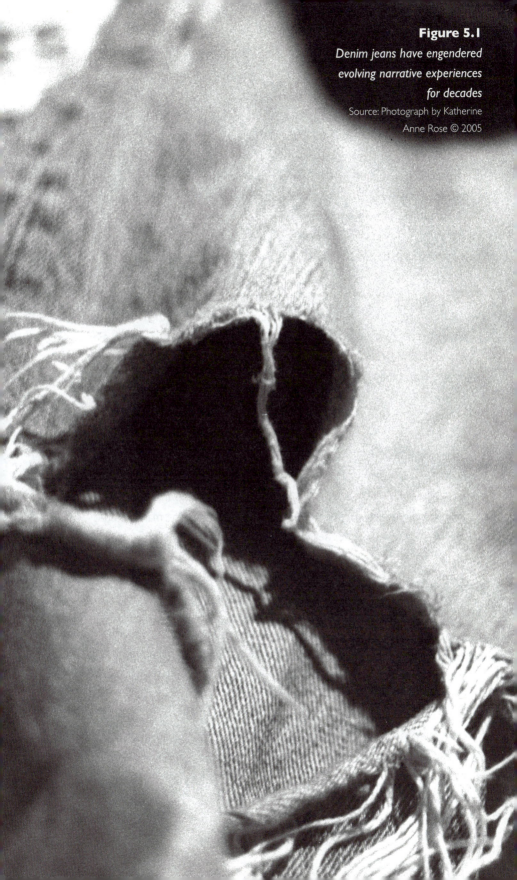

Figure 5.1
*Denim jeans have engendered
evolving narrative experiences
for decades*
Source: Photograph by Katherine
Anne Rose © 2005

Purchased like blank canvases, jeans are worked on, sculpted and personified over time. Jeans are like familiar old friends providing animated narrative to life – a repository of memories – mapping events as and when they occur. Like comfort blankets they feel and smell familiar. The character they acquire provides reflection of one's own experiences, taking the relationship beyond user and used to creator and creature. Similar in philosophy to the way in which voice recognition software sculpts itself around the phonic idiosyncrasies peculiar to a particular user, jeans become tailored to the physical individualities of the wearer to become a part of them.

To intensify the sense of creation further, people rip their jeans, cut them with knives, scrub them with a yard brush, bleach them and throw paint over them. One lady in New Jersey takes the notion of customization a step further by driving a pick-up truck over her pair, all to intensify and personalize the accumulation of patina. Second-hand pairs flaunting genuine wear and tear can even be purchased online, worn by real-life cattle herders, gold miners and a host of other rugged hands-on professionals. This fast mode of narrative adoption is sometimes referred to as acquired significance, and enables consumers to quickly slip into the life of another person, like a costume – an experience which is nurtured between user and object, but which can also be mediated effortlessly to the wider society through its descriptive semantic. Beyond the world of jeans, manufactured objects, in general, must endeavour to clearly express through their design a narrative that users can easily identify with, while also being able to discuss it with their peers. When narrative experiences are communicable in this way, the objects which deliver them adopt even greater significance; they share intimate narratives with the user, which can then be shared further within the user's social group.

The somewhat unusual narrative experiences served up by jeans are enjoyed by millions of people each year, and provide the cornerstone for a well-established and highly competitive industry. Yet, despite the continual introduction of new styles, cuts and fabrics, most consumers are content at keeping the few pairs they already have. Transient heroes such as jeans and houseplants side step obsolescence by possessing evolutionary characteristics; they evolve slowly and amorphously through use to keep the story alive. Unfolding narratives such as these map human and object relationships as and when they develop. Similar in many ways to a diary, they place events within a chronological context that is exclusive to the user. When the time eventually does come for replacement, brand loyalty is generally high. 'The most powerful and lasting benefit you can give a customer is an emotional one.'[12] Consumers develop empathy with these products, which viscerally nurtures empathy with the brand. Customers are subsequently kept loyal and market share is healthily sustained. 'Emotion is not something layered on by a stylist. In an aircraft seat it is as much part of its function that the traveller feel calm, relaxed and safe as it is fire resistant, ergonomic and accordant with safety regulations.'[13]

Leaving space for the user

Narrative experiences must not be over-programmed; spontaneous occurrences create the magic between the subject and the object; without them, relationships seldom supersede the banal. Over-programming is an inhibiting act that serves to sterilize outcomes, killing the romance by turning interaction into just another anonymous sequence of pre-planned events. To overcome this mode of interaction, it is vital that sufficient ambiguity is present, leaving space for the inclusion of the user psyche.

Into each discursive engagement between subject and object users introduce their own unique cocktail of preconceptions, beliefs and ideals. Users can be drawn into discourse by embedding emergent properties that only become visible through engagement. The design of appropriately ambiguous scenarios torments users into perceiving artefacts through their own individually polished looking glass, rendering the subsequent experience autonomous. Spontaneity, magic and intimacy can therefore be catalysed rather than planned through an object's ability to reflect or somehow echo the nuances of an individual user, like an existential mirror.

To an observer, the things we own and cherish may appear superfluous, 'banausic [mechanical or routine], even venal';[14] yet we cling to them because they have great and deep meaning for us. By allowing the healthy accumulation of narrative, profound sensations of attachment, empathy and even love may incubate. 'It is this empathy and, indeed, intimacy, between the subject and the object which activates numinous experiences and expands consciousness.'[15] Due, in large part, to the unique and highly ambiguous nature of engagement between people and things, narratives are solely exclusive to each individual user, and frequently give rise to acute emotional attachments so strong that the object in question may be considered irreplaceable.

The teddy bear factor

Swiss industrial analyst Walter Stahel discusses certain narrative phenomena in terms of their *teddy bear factor*. Despite the toy market's daily introduction of newer and fluffier bears, teddies the world over are faithfully loved, cherished and adored for literally decades on end. When an arm falls off, it is sewn back on; if an eye becomes loose, it is fixed. Most adults – if pushed – will confess to still owning at least one bear: a bear with a gender, name and age. More importantly, they will share a rich narrative history with the bear, elevating its often worn-out physical body to an irreplaceable plateau that is safely beyond the reach of obsolescence and waste. A new bear would not be the same; narrative of this intimate nature cannot be purchased and the many layers of emotional investment embedded in the old bear are impossible to replace or simulate. The innocent naivety of teddy bears undoubtedly provokes a deeper nurturing – an almost parental mode of attachment – that is both intimate and sustainable. Stahel utilizes this scenario as a metaphorical model that may be applied to both the analysis and design of practically any narrative possibility, from traditional garden furniture to the most contemporary Bluetooth Personal Digital Assistant (PDA).

Certainly, a deep human need drives the existence of narrative experiences such as bears, jeans and houseplants; the origin of this need, however, is less certain. These attachments constitute a substantial element of the 'self-development process of human beings'[16] and enable us to look upon the past self that we wish to cultivate. 'Material possessions are used as symbols of what we are, what we have been, and what we are attempting to become.'[17] As an information-saturated society, we are plugged into a myriad of narratives at any one given time. However, it is inaccurate to assume that a one-way flow of information should occur here. Consumption is a cybernetic process and narrative, therefore, may seldom

Figure 5.2

Teddies transcend obsolescence
by accumulating meaning
through time

Source: Photograph by Katherine
Anne Rose © 2005

be experienced via a one-way master and slave hegemony. Rather, the flow of information must flow in both directions and can be influenced or guided by subject or object, creator or creature. Consequently, false oppositions – such as consumer and consumed – can be misleading as they grossly oversimplify what is an intricate matrix of two-way, reflexive relationships.

As we pursue further meaning through objects our ideals change, and so the consumer quest for accurate reflections of a continually evolving self drives eternally forth. Until objects possess evolutionary capabilities enabling a co-evolution with the user, we will forever be growing a landfill of discarded objects whose only crime was failure to keep the story alive.

To cut a short story long

Most consumer products are like stories with an incredible opening line, but which just continue repeating it throughout. Their narrative capabilities are pathetically limited, usually possessing one cute trick that raises the eyelids of passing consumers to engage them in an almost flirtatious semiotic dialogue. Born of a somewhat narcissistic mindset, objects of this nature amaze from the shop window, but tragically leave nothing in reserve. Rejection – like rot – promptly sets in to forge colossal voids between the subject and the object.

Today's wastefully transient mode of consumption is not unlike the consumption of stories, movies, gossip and other social narratives. It too is a goal-orientated endeavour with a strong emphasis on uncovering the mystery, reaching the end and, ultimately, knowing all there is to know about a particular place, thing or occurrence. The Schumacher Society claim that quality of life 'is dependent on the number of stories we know about the items we use in our daily life'.[18] Therefore, to avoid unnecessary waste it is crucial that products are designed with a greater narrative stamina, enabling their stories to patiently unravel over a rewarding period of years rather than just a handful of fleeting days.

Storytelling

Storytelling is an ancient socio-cultural art practised by people of all cultures since the dawn of human history and it sustains meaningful cultural information through a rich archive of folklore, legend and other social narratives. Since early adapters evolved larger, more creative, brains capable of comprehending abstract imaginative ideas, human cultures have evolved in terms of both their complexity and richness. Even prior to the development of language, stories were depicted over generations via numerous mediums from ritualized dance to meticulously crafted illustrations on stone surfaces. By immortalizing both physical and spiritual encounters in this way, life experiences could be shared and rationalized amongst peers, enabling the cultivation of mutual understanding within social groups.

A captivating narrative must play on our deepest desires, dreams and fears in order to hold us in its grasp, enchanted and helpless. Like a puppeteer, an accomplished storyteller commands the psyche by artfully tweaking appropriate strings to cultivate subtle emotional responses within onlookers. Stories may flex and warp in reaction to audience feedback, allowing them to be tailored in real time, rendering storytelling a cyclic process of continual feedback and feed-forward. In *The Republic* Plato states: *everything that deceives may be said to enchant.* If we apply this philosophy to the design of narrative experiences, it becomes clear that both knowledge and understanding are agents of destruction. Durable narratives must therefore attempt to side step the deflowering gaze of the consumer, maintaining enchantment while never actually being fully understood.

In 1943 Jean Paul Sartre stated that 'to have seen through and therefore know is to deflower the entity'.[19] The uptake of products is largely motivated by this notion; we consume the unknown in order to demystify and make it familiar. Waste therefore appears to be as much a part of the consumption experience as are purchase and use. It is evolution made tangible. Simply recount the last domestic spring clean to recall sensations of lightness, betterment and fresh feelings of efficiency:

> The general movement of exudation (of waste) of living matter impels him, and he cannot stop it; moreover, being at the summit, his sovereignty in the living world identifies him with this movement; it destines him, in a privileged way, to that glorious operation, to useless consumption.[20]

Storytelling may also be deployed as an agent of memory, where abstract scenarios can be woven into known narrative sequences to assist in both the storage and recall of complex experiences. For example, the telephone number 64321684 might be tricky to remember without multiple revisions; yet if told that all the numbers are half the previous number – 64, 32, 16, 8 and 4 – it immediately becomes memorable for anyone who can divide by two. This technique of interlacing new data amongst existing knowledge is referred to (by cognitive psychologists) as *chunking* and is widely utilized by educators to ease the learning process. However, designers could also harness chunking as a means of making abstract virtual experiences more tangible and comprehensive.

As faster and more virtual genres of social interaction are developed, the popularity of traditional storytelling as a mediator of socio-cultural narratives is in rapid decline. This makes way for faster modes of pre-programmed material engagement in which anonymous narrative experiences are clumsily delivered via short, sharp bytes of one-way information – mass manufactured artefacts that hastily recount homogenized tales of technological genius and human accomplishment to a disenchanted audience of non-participatory users, projecting us forth into a disposable realm of superfluous materialism that is fuelled by a distinct lack of sustained interest in the stories being told.

The ecological impact resulting from this kind of alienation is variable and greatly scenario dependent. For example, a televised retrospective on the history of potato peeling in Belgium might simply provoke a lunge for the remote control with no real harm done. Conversely, when disinterest is allowed to gestate with manufactured objects themselves, the consequences can be both financially wasteful and ecologically hazardous. It is therefore imperative that narrative experiences are delicately planned to provide the user with sufficient time to build layers of emotional connection, while ensuring not to draw the experience out so long as to induce estrangement.

Domestic robotics

The fast-growing industry of domestic robotics is all too aware of the crucial role that narrative experiences play in the nurturing of durable subject–object relationships, particularly in developed parts of Asia such as Japan, Korea and Taiwan.

To assist in the perceptive clarity of these narratives, the industry has recently polarized itself into two distinctly separate genres of robots consisting of assistants and companions. Interestingly, robots falling into the assistant genre generally feature slick, anthropomorphic forms, while companion droids tend to be more abstract and frequently lend aesthetic attributes from the furry world of cute and cuddly. It is also worthy of note that the way in which we anthropomorphize domestic robots serves to illustrate the way in which we truly perceive our own existence as the following: 'anthropomorphization is a case of false referential exchange whereby man is equated with machine and machine becomes a signifier of humanity'.[21] As with almost any human-made creation, the dreams, desires and values of the maker – through the process of making – become deeply embedded within the object itself; mass-produced artefacts therefore provide a broader testimony to the dreams, desires and values of society as a collective whole.

Launched online in 1999, Aibo (*Artificial Intelligence roBOt*) falls boldly into the companion genre by taking on the gestalt appearance of a robot dog. Sony affectionately named their new litter of mechanized pups Aibo to incorporate the sound *ai*, meaning love in Japanese, while *aibo* means friend, indicating the kind of relationships to be expected from these strangely endearing hyper hounds. Aibo comes with six basic emotions – happiness, anger, sadness, dislike, fear and surprise – and four basic urges – to love, explore, move and be recharged – that begin to lightly scratch the complex surface of human behavioural ambiguity, though its emotional capabilities are still quite primitive. Despite the emotional attributes that permeate the Aibo family, they are still subconsciously pigeonholed by users as technological products and thus fall foul of the impatience and relentlessly increasing consumer expectations that befall other such hi-tech goods:

It is a very common late 20th-century phenomenon to think that we can purchase a commodity to give us the illusion of a full experience, while our experience is just an abstract of the real thing. For example, many people eat dinner at McDonald's and call it a meal.[22]

Several product generations later in 2001, the Aibo ERS-220 popped its head out of the Sony kennel, bringing with it a 75-word vocabulary and an onboard camera with which to take its own photographs. It also uses a combination of lights to both communicate its moods and express itself quite strongly to the owner. It can learn tricks and react to complex voice commands, and has numerous sensors enabling appropriate feedback in response to petting, or lack of petting, in the more neglectful cases. Furthermore, the nature of interaction that occurs between an ERS-220 and its owner shapes the growth of its character and temperament. To make things even more interesting, it cannot be reset and so must be lovingly raised from a naive pooch to a wise old hound. This places a certain parental responsibility on the owner's shoulders, coercing them to tread carefully and treat their new companion well in order to avoid ending up with an adolescent rogue instead of the subservient robo-pup so fondly dreamed of.

Needless to say, the narrative experiences that percolate from these relationships are both rich and individual, elevating human–object interactions onto a new and enlightened plateau. These often profoundly resonant experiences 'extol the virtues of those simple, yet ethereal, associations that make life joyous, that give meaning to our existence far beyond the conventional boundaries'.[23] However, Sony chose to provide owners with a shortcut in the form of a software programme that bypasses those lengthy adolescent years, granting more impatient users with the option to cut to the chase if desired. In so doing, the accumulation of precious narrative experience is also bypassed, making the intensity of the subsequent relationship between subject and object very much diluted.

When discussing autonomous products and the potential creation of objects that are in full possession of their own free will, it is worth remembering that there is nothing at all new or revolutionary about this:

> The technological object has always been a source of interest and fascination for culture. Soon after the discovery of electricity, the concepts of the robot and 'Frankenstein' were introduced to society by the literary world. Yet, the notion of animating the inanimate is not new and need not depend on circuits and batteries. The ancient Hebrew Golem and a thousand flying carpets

indicate that mankind's relationship with the physical has always contained far more than mere aesthetics or use-value.[24]

Written in a time of dramatic social and economic change – namely, the industrial revolution – Mary Shelley's *Frankenstein*[25] provides further evidence of this growing societal fear of scientific and industrial endeavours, fuelled partially by the inborn urge of our species to recreate itself:

> Frankenstein is distinctly related to the revolutionary period of 1780 to 1830 or the period of the first industrial revolution. There was a strong conviction in England, in the early Victorian times, that rapid future changes would take place and there were wide differences of view about the extent to which they would be beneficial.[26]

Shelley's novel presents a cautionary tale about the unforeseen outcomes of scientific research, though it may also be argued that 'Frankenstein can be read as a tale of what happens when a man tries to create a child without a woman.'[27]

In 1950, science fiction writer Isaac Asimov created his first collection of short stories entitled *I, Robot*, consisting of nine tales depicting the life of positronic androids. Within these tales can be found what he refers to as the *Three Laws of Robotics*, a three-point principle upon which robots may effectively function without posing any threat to humans. The three laws are as follows:

1. A robot may not injure a human being or, through inaction, allow a human being to come to harm.
2. A robot must obey the orders given it by human beings except where such orders would conflict with the First Law.
3. A robot must protect its own existence as long as such protection does not conflict with the First or Second Law.[28]

Asimov's trio of robotic laws serve to illustrate the degree of paranoia that surrounded the introduction of robots into the daily life of the 1950s, while also pointing out the broader suspicion that fully autonomous products would eventually revolt, turn on their human owners and, ultimately, seize control of the planet. In fact:

> Asimov developed the Three Laws (with the help of his editor John W. Campbell) because he was tired of the science fiction stories of the 1920s and 1930s in which the robots, like Frankenstein's creation, turned on their creators and became dangerous monsters. The positronic brains of Asimov's robots were designed around the Three Laws, so that it was impossible for the robots to function without them. There were enough ambiguities in the three laws to make for interesting stories; but there was only one story in the collection, *Little Lost Robot*, in which a robot posed any sort of danger to a human being.[29]

Asimov created the *Three Laws of Robotics* as a guarantee that the human species may continue to exercise dominance over their robotic counterparts. However, eventually an autonomous and free-thinking robot results from a manufacturing error, and begins to recognize its own superiorities over humanity.

Though a far cry from the cute and cuddly world of Sony's Aibo family, technophobian paranoia, such as that depicted in the work of both Asimov and Shelley, is still alive and well today – mediated widely through dystopian works of contemporary fiction, though also existing at the very forefront of day-to-day life through controversial scientific research into genetic reproduction and human cloning, around which orbits an equally disturbing measure of social dread.

Layers of narrative

The rate at which narratives unfold is as crucial as the narrative itself. If the development is too slow it will generate frustration, too fast and it will alienate the consumer through utter confusion. However, there are still further considerations lying beyond the temporal nature of narrative delivery. In particular, durable narrative experiences must embody multiple layers, enabling a number of co-dependent narratives – and sub-narratives – to be experienced simultaneously. Similar in ethic to a Russian doll, products could be designed to incorporate numerous layers of narrative neatly housed within each other that reveal, on discovery, not answers or grand finales but deeper and more complex layers. The result is an edgy stream of cliff hangers rather than the singular fast-food jolt provided by the majority of future trash designed today.

When speaking of alienation, German poet, playwright and theatrical reformer Bertolt Brecht claims that 'we don't want comfortable art, we want disruption'.[30] He saw continually punctuating disruptions as a highly effective means of maintaining a conscious connectedness between the viewer and the viewed, audience and performer – not unlike the way that MTV uses jolts to hold the audience's attention. A jolt or 'technical event'[31] is a sudden change in the direction of information flow. 'Public television boasts an average of 20 jolts per minute, 40 during commercial breaks, double what they were in 1978.'[32] At present, MTV is said to deliver around one jolt per second. The more jolts we are exposed to, the more likely we are to leave the remote control where it is; '[a] jolt forces your mind to pump for meaning'.[33]

An ancient Arabic legend named *A Thousand and One Arabian Nights* depicts a tale in which a beautiful young woman is lured into the tent of a murderous sultan. The sultan's original intention was simply to consume, then execute her. However, that night she artfully recounts the first part of a beautiful and mysterious tale. It is so compelling that he is unable to kill her since the story would not be continued the following night. As a result, the story goes on for 1001 nights, as does her life. This classic story – along with many others like it – is known as a frame tale, a story within a story. A frame tale is a sustainable narrative technique in which the main story is constructed in order to organize a collection of shorter stories. Narratives are discreetly packaged within other narratives, concocting wondrously rich narratives loaded with tension and complexity. Effectively authoring – or designing – frame tales can be complex and is somewhat of an art requiring a delicate balance of narrative logic spliced with a sense of edginess and uncertainty.

Narratives can also be utilized as agents of subversion, further enriching user–object relationships, keeping the interaction sufficiently ambiguous by delivering an ebb and flow of ever changing fictional realities that sustains enquiry. Perhaps more provocatively, narratives can challenge the way in which we live, consume and perceive the made world by masquerading as familiar, while secretly polluting the consumer psyche with subversive stories and ideas.

Smooth morphic shifts

Consumers cannot engage deeply with artefacts where there is no growth, no change, no narrative and only predictability. However, change alone alienates users though a lack of togetherness; therefore, a smooth and seamless shift must be present in order to evoke sensations of mutual growth. For example, if a storyteller were to continually switch stories every few lines, we would surely become lost and, consequently, experience alienation. If, however, the story is incrementally developed and grown, we engage passionately with it. Steadily unfolding narratives map the particular development of human–object relationships, thus closing the gap between self and other to create a unified experience. More importantly, users shape and influence the nature of narrative experiences by the very nature of interaction that occurs between two parties:

> With this form of design, the 'product' would be a fusion of psychological and external 'realities', [and] the user would become a protagonist and co-producer of narrative experience rather than a passive consumer of a product's meaning. The mental interface between the individual and the product is where the 'experience' lies.[34]

Users must therefore be designed into narratives as co-producers and not simply as inert, passive witnesses. 'The user becomes a protagonist and the designer becomes a co-author of the experience; the product creates dilemmas rather than resolving them'.[35] This process enables the nature of user interaction to shape the emergent narrative, creating perceivably one-off and individual experiences while ensuring the continued longevity of a given narrative experience.

Growing old gracefully

Each autumn – just like the last – arboreal-inclined onlookers crane their necks to enjoy the green canopy shift hue to rusty brown and sun-baked orange. The stout wooden limbs seem so impermeable; and yet, somehow, each year they amaze us all with their delicate and colourful displays, littering our streets and pathways days later with a scattering of crisp papery leaves. There is a curious beauty to be found in such transience: an urgency and a preciousness that compel us to hastily appreciate the spectacle before it is too late. But as anyone wearing corduroy flares will testify, everything – including fashion – moves in cycles: the changing of the seasons, the daily tag-team partnership of sun and moon and, of course, the fresh green leaves returning to the trees next spring.

Today – perhaps as a direct consequence of our streamlined and automated lifestyles – we seem to place ourselves beyond all this. Nature is frequently perceived as an opposing force, a random, unpredictable realm in constant rotation that must be beaten down and controlled. According to Georges Bataille, nature is widely perceived as an entity that could be likened to an unbroken horse that cannot be tamed. If we fail to train and suppress the wildness within the horse 'it is we who pay the price of the inevitable explosion'.[36] As though in reaction to these anxieties, we have learned how to convert natural resources – a term applied to matter for which we have a commercial use – into homogenous mass-produced materials. These materials enable us to easily and quickly manufacture vast quantities of products that are *built to last* and that *stand the test of time*. Repeated attempts to freeze out nature's inevitable decay has enabled us to develop a diverse palette of materials that are no longer recognizable to the micro-organisms and enzymes that degrade substances back to their basic nutritional building blocks. In doing so, we side step the degenerative glare of biological decay and now exist in a realm of relatively untouchable material immunity. 'We are on the brink of a materials revolution that will be on a par with the Iron Age and the industrial revolution. We are leaping forward to a new era of materials.'[37] Yet, despite the proto-durability of today's palette of materials, ageing still occurs and comes at an increasing cost to the environment, as ungraceful ageing is frequently the precursor to waste.

Interaction between subject and object – user and product – is not as fleeting and ephemeral as we might assume, nor is this interaction confined to the moments in which we are actually using something. The emotional and largely metaphysical interaction between subject and object occurs continuously, even when the two parties are absent from one another. The emotional interaction between a husband and wife, for example, does not grind to a halt simply because they are both at work; in their absence from one another throughout the working day, feelings, thoughts and the recalling of moments occupy their minds to ensure that although they are parted in a physical sense, emotionally they have been together all day. Back in the made world of interaction between people and things, we can see that this nature of continuous engagement – in a real sense – only takes place within the user, as products are not currently equipped with the degree of autonomy required to support such an emotional exchange. Although product-side evolution frequently takes place on a minor scale, at present these developments are generally of a derogatory and destabilizing nature.

If enduring narratives between emotionally demanding users and comparably inert products are to be nurtured, we as designers must look beyond objective considerations such as styling and ergonomics to consider deeper sensorial dimensions of objects. For example, the ageing properties of the materials we specify could be further exploited to engender new genres of objects and experiences in possession of evolutionary characteristics. This is not to say that everything should be made using wood, denim or, perhaps, leather; instead, provocative design concepts could emerge that challenge our social desire for a scratch-free world, illustrating how the onset of ageing could concentrate rather than dilute the *gestalt*. When ageing is embraced in this way, we can see that the transformative nuance of decay can be utilized by designers to great effect, ensuring that products are free to age and evolve gently through the course of time, rather than falling ruthlessly out of favour the moment their glossy façades of newness begin to peel away.

The accumulative process of ageing in products is inevitable. Whether we like it or not, things get old, and it is therefore important that we begin designing for desirable ageing, accepting mortality by embracing the inevitable fate that awaits all matter on this planet. That said, scratches, dints, stains, dints, knocks, gashes, chips, cracks and scrapes are generally perceived as derogatory manifestations whose presence serves to brutally scar an otherwise virginal landscape:

> This leads us straight to the issue of perfection. Numerous car owners polish their vehicle every week. It is the only way in which they can hold up the illusion of newness. Because perfection is vulnerable. A small scratch on a mudguard does more harm to a car than dismantling the engine.[38]

Products whose key design values lie in the degree of newness portrayed are especially vulnerable to the glare of decay, and designers need to start taking this notion more seriously. In designing perfection, you also design an unstable and highly vulnerable relationship between subject and object. The moment that fragile illusion of perfection falls under threat, so too does the relationship that is founded upon it.

Ageing material surfaces

The values affixed to the ageing of material surfaces are loaded with contradiction and are, at present, deeply genre dependent. Whether the steady build up of scars on a medieval oak floor or the withering gloss of a mobile phone chassis, patina plays a crucial role in both the mapping and portrayal of age and must come with carefully authored appropriateness to the genre if undesirable outcomes are to be avoided. Patina writes narrative into both the semiotic make-up and aggregate semantic of material experiences, holding great influence over the particular nature of the experiences that users are likely to perceive. During recent years, desirable patina has been largely dealt with as a bolt-on after thought, leading to the output of a stream of self-conscious and superficial whimsy, which assumes that the bearing of bumps and dints will somehow enhance user attachment.

If the presence of patina draws too much attention to itself, consumers will perceive the resulting experience as pre-programmed and inauthentic, ramming a colossal wedge between subject and object. In reality, sustainable narrative developments are complex and about far more than just the ageing of material surfaces, or a dint here and a scratch there. It is therefore imperative that patina is seen as a co-dependent element of the whole, rather than a one-stop approach to durable product design. Patina is, indeed, a potent addition to the designer's toolbox, but one that must be deployed with both subtlety and caution.

It is already commonly accepted that ageing surfaces can add character to objects, giving them a history, a sense of age and a story. Yet, more often than not, this ageing process devalues products by enforcing their sense of age and consequent loss of technological currency. Needless to say, this debilitating phenomenon is particularly prevalent within the digital product genre where – at present – the sole value indicators are focused almost exclusively on modernity. There are, of course, countless other product genres circulating the mainstream in which the accumulation of patina might afford objects with an elevated status that lifts them above the bland anonymity of a mass-produced world – patina which, through steady accumulation, provides signs of life, clues of use and other decipherable indications of an object's otherwise secret life. From grandma's walking stick with the worn handle to the key chipped paint around the car door handle, ageing material surfaces narrate tell-tale signs of life by embodying the user within the object.

Against the 'box-fresh' ideal

Popular design has a distinct preoccupation with producing 'box-fresh' experiences, objects that are at their absolute best when virginal and new. This means that both the intensity and cognitive value of product experiences will only deteriorate over time through a loss of what might best be described as freshness. The offspring of popular design are so finalized and complete as to leave no space for the user to incorporate their own identity, and any post-purchase alterations that do occur grate harshly against the existing overly programmed aesthetic. This approach to design can also estrange users from the process of creation by turning objects into nothing more than ornaments of utility. Utopian entities to be gazed upon such as art gallery exhibits are protected at all costs from the degenerative smudges and scuffs of an imperfect organic world. In any physical product scenario, the ageing process will occur as it always does; it is therefore crucial that products are designed to both accommodate and embrace their inevitable future. This way the onset of ageing will concentrate rather than dilute the *gestalt*, while reframing signs of age and overall product maturity as desirable consumer destinies.

Users occasionally step outside of their anonymous streamlined worlds into a stochastic consumer landscape inhabited by elite genres of temperamental, high-maintenance experiences. The maintenance requirements, and subsequent customization of objects within this genre, are often seen as the precursor to the generation of character, enabling them to somehow transcend their mass-produced identities by metamorphosing into something far more singular and charismatic.

Whether a temperamental vintage car, the woodworm-riddled legs and
faded lacquer surfaces of an antique dresser, or even the weathered
face of an elderly grandparent, the process of ageing frequently lends
an enduring charismatic quality to the experiential whole. 'The term
"character" neatly describes the meaningful content of an object when
consciously experienced.'[39] It must also be said that when technological
contemporaneousness is not the sole value designed into an object, its
resilience to superficial innovation fortifies by being equipped with other,
less transient, values.

Physical experiences that confidently flaunt the scars of age
without apology or justification adopt a notable degree of integrity that
enables them to grow old in a dignified manner. What may ordinarily be
seen as flaws somehow serve the contrary – affirming the authenticity of
an object's claims of age by subtly depicting a narrative to the particular
nature of its life. In a world where respect for our elders is a practically
universal doctrine, such behaviour is hardly surprising and signifies the
enduring human urge to engage in evolving, durable relationships within
a homogenized world. At present, product ageing is dealt with in deeply
genre-specific terms and therefore remains cautiously sequestered from the
bulk of mainstream design innovation. Indeed, products must be designed
to grow old gracefully; yet, with such a multitude of variables, the question
must be asked: is the sustainability of narrative experience really as simple
as a dint here and a scratch there?

Designing products with the capability to deliver enduring
narrative experiences is not simply a matter of appropriate material
specification, or selecting natural and transient materials such as denim or
wood as opposed to cold and often sterile polymers such as Acrylonitrile
Butadiene Styrene (ABS) or polycarbonate. On the contrary, narrative
experiences can be driven by a multitude of designable means of which
appropriate material specification is just one. Clearly, materials have a crucial
role to play in the ageing process, both in terms of their physical endurance
properties and social preconception. However, the social values affixed
to the ageing of material surfaces are intensely complex and somewhat
schizophrenic, to say the least. Natural fibre carpets age badly, while
pinewood floors are practically at their worst when new; and leather-bound
books improve like fine wines, whereas a conventional hardback appears

dog-eared and tatty. Despite these gross inconsistencies, patina is, indeed, a necessary – if not imperative – design consideration to assist the extension of product lifespans in graceful and socially acceptable ways.

Chapter summary

Beneath the silken skin of mass manufacturing, harsh contradictions dwell regarding the explicit nature of the newness that consumers actually desire.

. . . .

Objects capable of delivering durable narrative experiences already pollute the mainstream, though most remain cautiously quarantined within low-tech product genres.

. . . .

Consciousness is interpreted by consumers as the feeling that something has autonomy: a set of intentions based purely around one's particular existence, or something that seems to be in possession of its own free will or alterity.

. . . .

Objects that evolve slowly over time build up layers of narrative by reflecting traces of the user's invested care.

. . . .

JNDs define the amount that something must be altered in order for the difference to be perceivable.

. . . .

When consumers develop empathy with products, a visceral empathy is nurtured with the brand; customers are subsequently kept loyal and market share is healthily sustained.

. . . .

Narrative experiences must not be over-programmed; spontaneous occurrences create the magic between subject and object. Without them, relationships seldom supersede the banal. Spontaneity and magic should be catalysed rather than planned through an object's ability to echo the idiosyncrasies of each individual user.

. . . .

Most consumer products are like stories with an incredible opening line, but which just continue repeating it throughout. Their storytelling capabilities are pathetically limited.

. . . .

Transient consumption is not unlike the consumption of stories, movies and gossip; it, too, is goal orientated, with a strong emphasis on uncovering mystery and knowing all there is to know.

· ·

Durable narratives must side step the deflowering gaze of the consumer, maintaining enchantment while never actually being fully understood. Captivating narratives must play on our deepest desires, dreams and fears in order to hold us in their grasp: enchanted and helpless.

· ·

The pace at which narratives unfold is as crucial as the narrative itself; too slow, and it will generate frustration, too fast and it will alienate the consumer through utter confusion.

· ·

Durable narrative experiences must embody multiple layers, enabling a number of co-dependent narratives to be experienced simultaneously – revealing, on discovery, not answers or grand finales but deeper and more complex layers.

· ·

A frame tale is a sustainable narrative technique in which the main story is constructed in order to organize a collection of shorter stories, concocting rich narrative textures loaded with tension and complexity.

· ·

A smooth shift must occur; if a storyteller were to continually switch stories every few lines, we would surely become lost and, consequently, experience alienation. If the story is incrementally developed and grown, we engage passionately with it.

· ·

Users must be designed into object narratives as co-producers and not simply as inert, passive witnesses, a process that enables the nature of user interaction to shape the emergent narrative.

· ·

Patina writes narrative into both the semiotic make-up and aggregate semantic of material experiences, holding great influence over the particular nature of the experiences that users are likely to perceive. However, the values affixed to the ageing of material surfaces are loaded with contradiction and are, at present, deeply genre specific.

· ·

It is imperative that patina is seen as a co-dependent element of the whole, rather than a one-stop approach to durable product design. Patina is, indeed, a potent addition to the designer's toolbox, but one that must be deployed with subtlety and caution.

· ·

In any physical product scenario, the ageing process will occur as it always does. It is therefore crucial that products are designed to both accommodate and embrace their inevitable future. This way the onset of ageing will concentrate rather than dilute the *gestalt*, while reframing signs of age and overall product maturity as desirable consumer destinies.

A toolbox of ideas

Layers of narrative: durable narrative experiences must embody multiple layers, allowing numerous interwoven narratives to be simultaneously cognized and revealing, on discovery, not answers or grand finales, but deeper and more complex layers lurking even deeper within the object's semiotic make-up. Frame tales are helpful here, whereby a main story is constructed in order to organize a collection of shorter sub-stories, enabling the artful concoction of rich narratives loaded with tension and complexity.

. . . .

Producers not observers: when embedding narrative experiences within products, always perceive the user more as a co-producer of the narrative, rather than just a passive observer. This way, the narrative experience that does eventually unfold will be a unique experience since it has – to some degree – been shaped and produced by each unique and individual user.

. . . .

Pace: pay careful attention to the pace at which narrative experiences unfold; too slow and they will generate frustration, too fast and they will alienate the consumer through utter confusion. Ideally, pace should be varied, ensuring that an air of uncertainty circulates the object, while also optimizing the sense of anticipation to nurture an intense connectedness between subject and object.

. . . .

Ageing gracefully: anticipate the ageing process of objects. Whether we like it or not, things get old, and it is imperative that we begin designing for desirable ageing as a means to embrace their inevitable futures. This is not to say that everything should be made using wood, denim or, perhaps, leather; rather, provocative design concepts must emerge that challenge our social desire for a scratch-free world, illustrating how the onset of ageing could actually concentrate rather than dilute the *gestalt*.

chapter six

de-fictioning utopia

The problem with utopia

In 1516 British writer Thomas More created what he called *Utopia*,[1] an uncomplicated vision of an apparently flawless future depicted via an imaginary island that enjoyed the greatest perfection in politics, law and all other aspects of life. Alhough fictional, More's text emerged from a very real disenchantment with his life in 16th-century England. Of course, utopias such as this seldom find their way into conventional reality; yet they play a key societal role by illustrating the direction in which we may collectively face, while raising pertinent questions regarding the social values that underpin these idealist visions of the future.

In describing our societal preoccupation toward casting utopian visions of the future, social activist Jeremy Rifkin – in his revolutionary work entitled *The End of Work: The Decline of the Global Labor Force and the Dawn of the Post-Market Era* – states that:

> Every society creates an idealized image of the future – a vision that serves
> as a beacon to direct the imagination and energy of its people. The Ancient
> Jewish nation prayed for deliverance to a promised land of milk and honey.
> Later, Christian clerics held out the promise of eternal salvation in the heavenly

kingdom. In the modern age, the idea of a future technological utopia has
served as the guiding light of industrial society. For more than a century utopian
dreamers and men and women of science and letters have looked for a future
world where machines would replace human labour, creating a near workerless
society of abundance and leisure.[2]

In this respect, utopias are imaginary places considered to be perfect or
ideal; they are destinies to be chased and futures to be pursued. For an
onward-facing species such as us, utopias are vital; they free us from the
shackles of an imperfect present by revealing a limitless world of imaginable
futures, providing us with hope, optimism and, essentially, a reason
to continue.

  Yet, as with all things, utopias possess a dark side. They set up
unrealistic expectations, generate false hope and, ultimately, foster a restless
culture of perpetual disenchantment with the now. In this respect utopias
are antagonistic; their immaculate renderings of the future merely serve
to point out the otherwise unnoticed deficiencies of our present lives by
repeatedly taunting us with glossy portrayals of how things could, should
and ought to be. Over the last century the concept of utopia has steadily
crept its way into almost all aspects of modern life. Today, the societal
thirst for visions of a perfect future is insatiable, frequently deployed like an
umbilical chord to sustain demand-nurturing industries such as advertising,
marketing and design. In consequence, the orientation of individual utopias
is steadily becoming more and more prescribed. After all, 'utopias are
supposed to be places where everyone is happy; but conflicts over what
constitutes happiness are almost inevitable. Getting everyone to agree
on how to be happy becomes an effort at social engineering that risks
becoming totalitarian control.'[3] This is another trap presented by utopias:
they streamline culture into one approved version, snuffing out creativity,
diversity, individuality and spontaneity in the process.

Design is utopian

The current model of technocentric design is in danger of falling into the
trap discussed above by producing streams of objects that signify utopian
values founded upon a single prescribed and socially approved version of

reality. In so doing, material culture becomes inadvertently homogenized into one popular version, forming a monoculture that embodies only one vision of the future, one utopia: a utopia that has us all sitting around – jobs done – with nothing to do but surf eBay in search of further utopian materialism. Meanwhile, a gentle background noise of bleeps, hums and clicks serves to remind us that our products are at work and all is, indeed, well on the home front. 'Perhaps the centralized system that led to such a suffocating monoculture was a historic anomaly, an artefact? The technology of the phonograph, radio and television demanded centralization.'[4]

New genres of design must develop – beyond the centralized world of lighter, faster, smarter – which adopt a more critical stance, creating challenging and provocatie portrayals of the future, delivering numerous conflicting projections of tomorrow, which through their existence illustrate that there is more than one way to live your life:

> Instead of thinking about appearance, user-friendliness or corporate identity, industrial designers could develop design proposals that challenge conventional values … new strategies need to be developed that are both critical and optimistic, that engage with and challenge industry's technological agenda.[5]

The values signified in mass-manufactured objects need to develop a more provocative edge, diversifying to incorporate elements of fantasy, hyper-reality and fiction. They need to provide a rich critique of our present situation through objects that deliver alternative social, cultural, economic, political, environmental and technological values to enable the exploration of numerous alternative realities to the one so frequently put forward by conventional design.

Fiction

Fiction is based on the imagination and not necessarily on fact; it facilitates the founding of fantastical narratives depicting alternative realities, often laced with a healthy dose of utopian idealism or, indeed, dystopian doom and gloom. Fictional narratives abound – whether epic tales of romance such as Margaret Mitchell's *Gone with the Wind*,[6] or apocalyptic fantasies such Philip K. Dick's *Blade Runner*,[7] George Orwell's *1984*[8] or

William Gibson's *Neuromancer*.[9] Although the aforementioned works may be compelling, fiction does not simply exist for the sole purpose of entertainment and is more than just a literary genre or category of movie *per se*. Fictions perform a vital role by weaving rich narrative threads throughout our daily lives, which we may cling to and engage with on both emotional and rational levels; they serve to illustrate our innermost fears, anxieties, desires and hopes as a societal collective.

Fictitious narratives also provide an invaluable resource of consumable experiences; although not overly concerned with truth, fiction is not a dishonest medium: it simply manipulates notions of the possible, the real and the seemingly unreal. It may be said that 'in our predominately materialist culture we take it for granted that the physical world is real. But in what sense are experiences, thoughts and feelings real?'[10] When consuming fictional narratives, their absence from reality becomes unimportant as the physical and emotional experience of engaging with fictions is very real; they powerfully stimulate and agitate our curiosities and we are compelled, tantalized and mystified by them. Furthermore, unlike utopia, the term *fiction* makes no value judgements, and merely denotes versions of reality that may be experienced, which are not necessarily better or worse than the norm. Fiction may also exist in the now, and therefore possesses an immediacy that facilitates the creation of today's experienced consumable realities.

Fiction may be found in countless aspects of life, and its reach far exceeds the leisure-time domains of bookstores and movie theatres. In the world of goods, consumable fictions from the bizarre to the banal proliferate, purveying fictitious renderings of reality from deep within the semantic layers of objects. The embedding of consumable fiction within product semantics is commonplace and can be found – on some level – in almost all product scenarios. For instance, refrigerators' gloss-white façades fictionalize a cleanliness that is not actually there; air intakes on the side panels of a BMW Z1 spin the fictional yarn of a high-performance, beast-like motor panting for breath; while the handles on the corners of a G4 Mac create a fictitious caricature of nomadic urban mobility.

Although it is quite obvious that these fictions have been designed into a given product semantic, this fact remains somehow irrelevant to

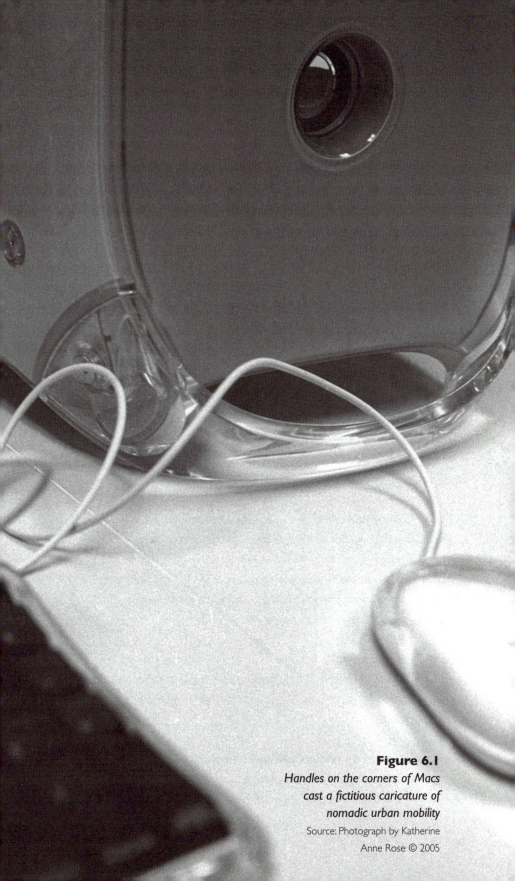

Figure 6.1
*Handles on the corners of Macs
cast a fictitious caricature of
nomadic urban mobility*
Source: Photograph by Katherine
Anne Rose © 2005

us as consumers – just as we know a fictional literary work may have been similarly conceived, linked to reality only through metaphor or other abstract means. Our desire to explore and consume fictions as perceived in objects bears strong similarities to the way in which we might consume a fictional movie, play or novel; the emphasis is not on authenticity or truth, but on experience and meaning.

The need for fiction

Fictional objects possess a restless quality that consumers find impossible to leave unattended, and this is hardly surprising. The endeavours of industrialization have steadily transformed post-modern culture into a hands-off experience where practically everything is done for us. The questions have been answered, the problems have been solved and mysteries are demystified. Through our own genius we have incrementally stripped the world of its charm and mystery; by relentlessly peeling back layers of the unknown we uncover truths, which somehow nullify the otherwise enchanting world in which we live. Just as the sight and sound of a thunderstorm no longer connects us with an outraged god, with knowledge and certainty follows a deadening silence as there are no more questions to be asked and no further fictions to pursue:

> Corporate futurologists force feed us a 'happy-ever-after' portrayal of life where technology is the solution to every problem. There is no room for doubt or complexity in their techno-utopian visions. Everyone is a stereotype, and social and cultural roles remain unchanged. Despite the fact that technology is evolving, the imagined products that feature in their fantasies reassure us that nothing essential will change, everything will stay the same.[11]

As everyday life continues to become more and more programmed, the need for fiction, complexity and dialogue increases exponentially. For today's comatose consumer, fiction is no longer a question of need but one of absolute necessity.

Consumption is a process of de-fictioning

Most products provide us with a utopian, idealized and slightly fictional view of how the world could be; they are fictional in that they depict imagined futures – alternative versions of reality – that users feel compelled to pursue and engage with. Yet, the alternative realities mediated by these objects are mere glimpses: fleeting moments of experience that are short lived to say the least. Products must therefore possess richer, lengthier and more complex fictions if the consumption process is to be both satisfying and longer lasting. In this light, the process of consumption may be reframed as a process of de-fictioning the world since once fictions are explored, demystified and known, the debate essentially ends and new fictions are sought.

The desire to pigeonhole and categorize is destructive, stripping potential experiences of their individuality and freshness. Products must resist categorization to keep the debate alive and maintain a tantalizingly fictional existence. Indeed, de-fictioning is an apocalyptic process of serial destructions that must be avoided at all costs. An object must sustain its fiction to continually engage the user; if not, fictions will be found elsewhere.

Deflowering

New and consequently unfamiliar products radiate mysterious enigmatic qualities that quickly crumble away once familiarity begins to accumulate between the user and the object. Sartre refers to this existential mode of being as the *deflowering*[12] of an entity. Deflower is a somewhat dated literary or poetic term, meaning to deprive a woman of her virginity or, less commonly but more literally, to 'strip a piece of land of its flowers'.[13] Notice in these two descriptors the words *deprive* and *strip*; both indicate an involuntary submission imposed by an outside force. In the context of subject–object engagement, it is clear to see how Sartre's notion of deflowering may assist the framing of what is a fairly complex metaphysical exchange. The uptake of products is motivated, in part, by this notion of deflowering. We consume the unknown in order to demystify and make familiar, similar to the way in which we might wade through the pages of an Agatha Christie who-done-it in search of a villain to end the mystery. The process of consumption is as much about the journey – or process – as it is the final destination. In addition, consumption is a transformative process through which we grow and evolve in reaction to the experience of engaging with objects, though in the case of most consumer goods this journey is both monotonous and brief.

The value of meaning – and the rebirth of meaning – may be illustrated through its self-renewing ability to continually enrapture. As discussed earlier, consumption is a process in which we attempt to know, familiarize and, thus, outgrow the wonders of the artefact. Sartre refers to this manner of knowledge seeking as 'a deflowering of the entity'.[14] Transient meaning would ensure that the consumer's attempts to deflower – and therefore know – continue on as the object of consumption is never actually the same thing. In so doing, the journey – or process – of consumption continues healthily on.

Sustaining fiction

For an object to continually portray a fictional *gestalt* it must first be in possession of an ability to conceal, holding a few cards up its sleeve in order to avoid total discovery – keeping its distance by holding a part of itself back and, like a drip-feed mechanism, releasing subtle layers of meaning at steady intervals throughout the slow passing of time. The importance of holding something back may be illustrated through the childhood experience of eating a cake with a coin hidden somewhere within. The process of consumption is kept alive with anticipation and, consequently, is quite impossible to halt as the next mouthful might just be the one. The importance of this phenomenon is illustrated the moment the coin is discovered: the emotional intensity of interaction from that point forth steadily diminishes due to the realization that all has, indeed, been revealed. The once captivating and slightly enchanting cake is instantly relegated to the status of *just another cake*. The same may be said of mass-manufactured products in that something significant is lost the moment the extent of an object's features and functions has been fully explored and encountered.

The majority of user experiences – even those of a high intensity – will fade through time as users become accustomed to the stimulation provided. Having repeatedly experienced all the features and functions offered by a given product, there is literally nowhere left to go. It is usually at this point – and seldom prior to it – that users begin to consider upgrades, adaptations and other operational modifications to their now de-fictioned artefact in a vein attempt to restore, or somehow revive, the fiction that once proliferated.

Although exceptions to every rule will always exist, it may be said that even intense user experiences will potentially fade simply through excessive repetition and the subsequent nurturing of familiarity. The glare of de-fictioning therefore falls upon all objects that fail to sustain a degree of enchantment and mystery. Products possessing overly programmed semantics – or *perfect* products – are particularly vulnerable to the glare of de-fictioning. This is because they are too black and white, too easy to map and pigeonhole; in so doing, they leave little or no room for that crucial whiff of ambiguity that so often sustains the dialogue between subject and object. The challenge, therefore, is to blur the boundaries between the real and the fictional, while provoking a mode of mental consumerism that invites users to engage with sophisticated questions and ideas through everyday objects.

Consciousness

Deeper and more intense bonds are forged between users and objects when products portray a perceivable sense of consciousness. This is not to say that objects should literally be conscious; but, rather, a given object may react to its surroundings with an ontological receptiveness and flexibility of judgement that creates the impression of (or simulates) consciousness. In so doing, a world of richly diverse, amorphous and less predictable interactions unfolds, enabling far richer and more enduring engagements from within the regular confines of contemporary material culture. In addition, fictional characteristics often manifest in conjunction with the embedding of consciousness, as the degree of alterity portrayed by the object is notably higher, while the product's degree of self-awareness also affords a greater diversity and pluralism in feedback, which, in turn, creates a richer and more fictional palette of subject–object interactions:

> Alterity relations are the dimension of an interaction in which the object of one's intention is perceived in terms of otherness. This particularly elusive concept could be described as the felt sensation of the interaction with an autonomous or intelligent object, animal or individual.[15]

Alterity is frequently interpreted by the consumer as the feeling of something that has autonomy: a set of intentions based purely around one's own particular existence – something that seems to be in possession of its own free will.

Products should respond to a greater diversity of triggers than just on/off switches, volume controls, buttons, knobs and dials; in theory, products and their remote controls do not even need to be prodded and poked in order to function. It is plausible and interesting to conceptualize a range of products triggered simply by immediate environmental stimuli, such as air temperature, proximity to walls, proximity to user, local brightness, time of day/year or global positioning. We have become so over-familiarized and preconditioned to the push-button world of on and off that it feels quite bizarre simply imagining it as being any other way. Yet, it is this over-familiarization that is holding us back, both as a creative industry and as a society of forward-facing consumers. One example of this would be the camera.

Despite continual technological development, the 'say cheese' relationship that we have with cameras has evolved relatively little over the last few decades. Even today, with digital cameras sprouting out of mobile phones, Personal Digital Assistants (PDAs) and a growing number of other portable electronic objects, the way in which we interact with and functionally *take* pictures remains unchanged. The result is the all too familiar collection of rigid and self-conscious shots that usually follow any given family holiday, day trip or notable event – images that tend to result from attempting to capture reality with a push-button camera. Has the camera really evolved, or is it just quicker and easier to use now than it was before?

It is vital that designers begin to explore alternative renderings of product evolution beyond the prevailing technocentric model that clumsily whitewashes the creative industries today. What if cameras were triggered by sudden fluctuations in heart rate – and were tripped in sync with these fluctuations – far beyond the conscious control of users? The resulting photographs would provide alternative depictions of events based on emotional responses to given stimuli, a process that may be likened to human memory. Cameras would immediately become windows into the secret emotional lives of others; viewing the post-holiday snaps might uncover some revelatory truths about what really made you tick. If one's dog were to wear one of these cameras it might be something of a revelation to experience what makes them excited. Of course, ideas such as this serve mainly to demonstrate a point; their values lie in their ability to critically illustrate, rather than any commercial viability or immediate market worth.

Simulated consciousness can also be embodied by means of knowledge-acquiring systems or learning systems. In these instances, consumable consciousness deploys itself as a provocateur; acquiring information about a particular user, which is then used to 'detourn their assumptions',[16] sustaining the two-way dialogue by keeping it alive and thriving. In other words, the product must develop knowledge of user patterns in order to jolt them and respond to them in a reactionary manner.

The ultimate aim is to deploy simulated consciousness as an agent of discourse, rather than streamlined efficiency (as is commonly the case), broadening the discursive relationship between human and object to encourage the nurture of pluralism in subject–object encounters. The need for this manner of engagement is exemplified rather well by the increasingly popular experience of doing your weekly food shopping via the web. Beyond the relative stealth of online shopping and its obvious advantages, such as affordable home delivery, removal of the lengthy queuing process and an end to the wrestling of trolleys with minds of their own, online food shopping may have long-term detrimental effects. Due to the way in which most supermarkets have defined their web presence, shopping behaviour becomes incrementally streamlined over time. Websites present users with the time-saving option to simply repeat last week's shopping in a single click which, despite convenience, streamlines our eating habits while stripping away the diversity and variety that we, as a species, so dearly depend upon. Of course, supermarket sites will develop a unique user profile for each and every one of their customers and use it to make product recommendations based on what their market research tells them the customers will probably like. Other forms of internet shopping deploy this strategy. Amazon, for example, will recommend books – with a fairly shocking degree of accuracy – purely on the basis of your recent buying history.

Back in the world of subject–object interaction, an equally streamlined and experientially debilitating process is in effect. Mass-manufactured products possess a similarly repetitive model of interaction, which streamlines engagement through the passing of time until users are barely aware of what they are doing. Products perform their tasks well, maybe too well? Tools that begin to explore the simulation of consciousness such as artificial intelligence and artificial life are all too frequently discussed in terms of their ability to remove the decision-making process from humans. Refrigerators that email an automatically updated shopping list to the supermarket or *smart* bins that separate rubbish into predetermined recycling categories all contribute to the streamlining and 'dumbing down' of the species. These are dangerous commercial practices to cultivate: by removing the decision-making (or thought) process, they inadvertently homogenize society into an ever more programmed, predictable and mono-cultural mass.

Through an individually polished looking glass

We bring our own trolley load of psychological baggage into the meaning-consumption loop. This is why material engagements can seem so personal to us; meaning, therefore, appears to possess a highly diverse omnipresence. For example, a mass-produced black ceramic sphere will provoke quite different emotional responses from a Russian caviar farmer than it might from British snooker legend Steve Davis. The object is the same, but the response is anything but. This point may be further exemplified by the forging of attachments; though they can be catalysed in a number of ways, emotional attachments are particularly tricky to engineer. After all, 'for personal reasons one can feel emotionally attached even to a turnip or a hubcap'.[17] Each individual end user is in possession of their own unique archive of memories and personal meaning, which plays a key role in accumulating further meaning by affording even the most banal objects with powerfully transformative properties. This enables them to effortlessly transcend their former predispositions to become vigorous symbols of the self and carriers of great personal significance. 'No man ever looks at the world with pristine eyes. He sees it edited by a definite set of customs and institutions and ways of thinking.'[18] In this respect, it is fairly simple to see how each of us views the world – both made and unmade – through our own individually polished looking glass. It is important that designers learn to embrace these common idiosyncrasies, deploying them as agents of sustained fiction, since they serve to keep the dialogue alive and thriving between subject and object.

Frequently, the purpose of our consumption actually centres on the notion of an emergent property that only becomes visible through discursive engagement. Is it accurate, therefore, to speak of a product as being able to possess meaning? Surely a product or any other assemblage of matter is only capable of 'absolute signification',[19] or the driving of sensations within the perceiver or consumer? In this respect, false oppositions such as consumer and consumed are misleading, not to mention oversimplifying what is actually a highly complex assemblage of relationships. Such simplifications assume a one-way flow of information and possess an anthropocentrism that hinders the development of consensual agreement. Consumption is a cybernetic and polemical process embodying a need for co-dependence and mutuality; we do not consume matter, we engage with it, nor do we consume a world of information, we relate to it.

Designing products that mystify users through the presentation of fuzzy interfaces or spontaneous interactive jolts is entry-level practice and, therefore, relatively straightforward to achieve. Yet, although the felt sense of fiction can so easily be projected through designed objects, it is far more complex and problematic for designers to influence what happens after this initial projection. In experiential terms, the transformative character of sustained engagement that unfolds between people and things can only be loosely directed by designers, set off in the right direction and guided within fairly broad emotive parameters. This is due to the arbitrariness of human memory and its influence over the uniqueness of each end user's prior experiences, experiences that powerfully influence the way that they – as individuals – experience a world of manufactured objects and experiences.

Subjective interpretations of fictional artefacts will, at all times, show anomaly as users view objects through individually polished lenses. What some users view as a rich fictional narrative laced with enchanting nuances of uncertainty and dilemma, other users will experience simply as ambiguous and ill-defined rubbish. It is therefore particularly unrealistic for designers to boldly assume that the nature of the relationships that users establish with their design offspring may – in all cases – be finitely directed and governed, such as a well-crafted musical or art house movie. When bold and provocative statements are made, some people are simply not going to get it. It is for this reason that conventional design steers clear of the provocative and is, consequently, relegated to a servile packager of emergent technologies. Corporate pressure has designers creating anonymous artefacts in a range of colours designed to please every single user without exception; any deviation from this tried-and-tested path is simply deemed as unprofessional. At this point we can see that designing for empathy may never find its way into the mainstream – nor would it want to; it prefers to locate itself in the uncomfortable territory situated between art and design, providing an experientially rich alternative to the oftentimes bland model of material engagement with which we have become so habituated.

Phantile drives

Designers are actually meaning-makers. Just as a chef might add a minute trace of balsamic vinegar to a reduced tomato sauce, the designer is continually seasoning and adding depth to the consumable experiences driven by designed objects and experiences. In the context of consumer products, we will refer to each of these flavours as a *phantile drive* (PD). PDs are like hidden motors – or meaning-makers – deeply embedded within any given product's semiotic make-up. They are flavours waiting to be tasted and sensations awaiting the senses. Upon activation (perception), a PD will reveal itself, forcing the mind of the perceiver to pump for meaning. It is for this reason that the drives are described here as phantile since they are largely unseen. PDs are silent meaning generators that render matter meaningful – mirrors raised at random moments during interaction, enabling the consumer to view brief flashes of their own particular existence.

We pick up brief reflections of self and identity through PDs buried deep within a product's layers of signification. A PD is like a motor that generates meaning once perceived, and is phantile in the sense that it

Figure 6.2
*Unwanted appliances spend
a year or so of conscience
time in a cupboard prior to
being chucked*
Source: Photograph by Katherine
Anne Rose © 2005

is both metaphysical and deeply suggestive. As discussed earlier, each of us perceives these drives through a unique and individually polished looking glass, which adds further to the inherent spontaneity of the PD itself. Within any product, the PDs are already set in place; all that is needed to activate that awaiting network is the unsuspecting user.

As users we are subconsciously intertwined within an immeasurable number of meaning networks at any given time and remain largely unaware of their presence in our lives. In a physical sense, PDs do not necessarily exist, dwelling instead on a phenomenological level of interactivity in which considerations of objective reality are not necessarily taken into account. Once discovered, a PD will be revisited with the consumer expectation of a repeat performance. Premeditated reward-seeking behaviour such as this is universal to our species and can be found in most forms of interaction. At first we might see this pattern simply as learning: the natural development of knowledge that occurs as a direct result of interacting with the world. The Apple Power Mac G4 Cube possesses a great example of this.

The G4 Cube

The Apple Power Mac G4 Cube carries a multitude of PDs on board; some are more immediately apparent than others and one PD, in particular, gives rise to a fairly complex series of questions. Upon the minimalist surface of the G4 Cube there is a dormant ice-blue light beneath which is a proximity sensor that activates the bulb each time an object draws within a few millimetres of it. At first we might simply brand this as whimsical nonsense; it is not even that clever. Yet, for users, the light commands a richer discourse as the G4 Cube takes on a perceivable consciousness at this moment: an ontological awareness that greatly transcends the previous clumsy relationship of actual touch activation. Something far deeper appears to be going on here that resembles consciousness, awareness and, perhaps, even prescience. The experience that results from the activation of this PD delivers a kind of jolt and it fascinates us; like a purring cat the G4 Cube – in a very literal way – displays feedback to our gestures by acknowledging our presence. A degree of empathy is immediately forged and the relationship between user and object is subsequently bumped up a notch on the durability scale.

Once discovered, the neon glow of the G4 Cube will be revisited time and time again; unfortunately, with each visit the wonderment decreases slightly as the PD simply ceases to jolt. Once knowledge is allowed to develop, predictability – like rot – sets in and the once awe-inspiring PD now reeks of monotony and inevitability. The result is that from this point forth the user quickly loses conscious interest in the PD and, consequently, ceases to revisit it through lack of reward. And so the story ends.

The light is, of course, only one of a number of PDs embedded within the G4 Cube. The crucial point here, though, is that we have just witnessed the consumption of meaning. This is not to say that the PD is no longer active; it simply means that it is no longer active for that particular person as knowledge and familiarity have effectively 'deflowered the entity'.[20] Despite the sophisticated and quirky trigger mechanism of the G4 Cube's light, peppering objects with an array of blinking light emitting diodes (LEDs) will not radiate meanings of any lasting worth. And though this approach to design may initially turn heads, those heads will turn away with a similar haste since this kind of stimulus lacks sufficient depth to satisfy the perpetual consumer thirst for fresh, new experiences.

Omnipresent phantile drives

PDs are frequently deployed to generate eye-opening jolts and quirky surprises, like the *hello* greeting on a HIFI display. Gimmicks such as these exemplify one way of working with PDs. They deliver an opening jolt of reasonable intensity, yet somehow fail to sustain wonderment through the passing of time due – once again – to the PDs' inability to sustain its fiction by continually growing and evolving. In the case of the G4 Cube, Apple would view these tricks as a fantastic way of selling more units while guaranteeing a carefully forecasted obsolescence that makes way for the next generation of multicoloured 'must haves'. In advocating this doctrine, large corporations are failing to consider the impact that repeatedly disappointing their customers will have on the brand as a whole. These factors place the possibility of customer loyalty and repeat sales in jeopardy as they gestate lasting negative consumer perceptions of a given brand.

It is crucial that we – as a forward-facing industry – learn to see beyond initial sales targets and address deeper issues of product longevity.

One thing is certain: inert PDs are incapable of sustaining a relationship. They deflower quickly and therefore have no real life expectancy. The drives must embody amorphousness, an omnipresence enabling them to continually dance around the deflowering gaze of the user while deceptively concealing their entirety.

When speaking of deception, Plato believed: 'everything that deceives may be said to enchant'. If we apply this philosophy to the designing of PDs, we can see that both knowledge and understanding are to be considered agents of destruction. Therefore, PDs must attempt to side step the deflowering gaze of the consumer, maintaining enchantment while never actually being discovered. Enchantment itself may be managed in numerous ways; however, the art of deception and surprise might well be the most potent delivery system in this instance. As discussed earlier, the ability of a given product to continually amaze is largely subject to its intrinsic ability to conceal, holding a few cards up its sleeve as it were, in order to avoid total discovery and to subsequently stay ahead of the game.

To date, enchantment has been dealt with largely as a means of selling units, giving products a fantastic *trick*, which – like a magician – commands wonderment within onlookers. However, this one-trick approach to product design is of a dangerously short-term nature and is certainly not psychologically or emotionally durable. It creates great disillusionment and disappointment within users and generates animosity within the subject. To repeatedly enchant, a product must first possess an ability to grow and change. If anything, a product's ability to enchant must increase not decrease. Having it in your life should be a rich and fruitful journey, an unfolding process of punctuated revelations, each one more personalized than the last – creating a feeling of co-dependency, mutual growth and absolute togetherness.

Omnipresence may be exemplified well by the PD that delivers the jolt in a jack in the box. Its single function can never be effectively predicted; it even uses the guise of a clown to intensify the notion of deception. Yet, despite having only one clear function, a child will sit for hours enduring shock after shock without experiencing any disillusionment or alienation. This is because the jack in the box utilizes fiction. It is a deceiver whose secret lies in the unpredictability of an apparently predictable behaviour. It is almost impossible to predict, as each time you wind it up the resulting jolt will – almost always – come at a slightly different time. By continually nurturing uncertainty within the user, the jack in the box captures the full attention of the onlooker. This is a relationship founded on unpredictability and partial – or fuzzy – control. The PD may therefore be described as possessing a perceivable omnipresence, like a computer game that you cannot quite complete but which keeps you caught within the tantalizing hook of consuming it, and consuming it. In short, omnipresence allows a PD to function, but without ever being wholly understood or de-fictioned by the user.

Omnipresent PDs situate consumer consciousness deeply within both immediate and intuitive loops of control and feedback; the game of ping-pong illustrates this notion well. In ping-pong, the phenomenon of procedural growth – or learning – is particularly prevalent. Once in progress the game quickly becomes an anticipatory dialogue between two players, the ball's trajectory representing an information flow with a jolt occurring each time it is struck. Like an improvisational dance, both players attempt to flex and sway, reacting to one another, keeping the motion alive and the dialogue thriving. The overall concept of ping-pong is, of course, to overcome one's opponent; yet the unpredictability that underlies the actions of the other seems to guarantee the sustainability of the game by keeping the interaction sufficiently varied.

With novelty comes a voyage into the unknown, a disrobing of the mystery that surrounds it and the consumption of the unfamiliar. As described in *Information Theory*,[21] when discussing noise, 'at what point does music become noise?'[22] If a monotonous tone is allowed to continue unchanged, we withdraw attention from it and – on an unconscious level of cognition – the noise disappears. The PDs embedded within the semantic layers of products must also vary the jolts they deliver if they are to avoid predictability and the subsequent withdrawal of the user's attention span. In today's overburdened world of people and things, it is rare to witness such mutual interaction as the majority of products purvey monosyllabic personae, which promptly transform wonder and enchantment into drudgery and frustration. What we really crave are evolutionary relationships: two-way engagements that enable the self to continually perceive its own image through an ever evolving mirror.

155

Space

The designing of omnipresent PDs may be further facilitated by incorporating a measure of openness – or space – within product semantics, enhancing the degree of self that may be invested into the discursive engagement between subject and object. The term *space* is used here in the Taoist sense, in which space might denote a positive and much valued presence of nothing, rather than the Western concept of space denoting a negative absence or void-like emptiness. It is what shadow is to light and silence to noise. The key point here is that space does not mean *nothing*. For example, Japanese audiences, when attending a classical concert, remain silent during the quiet pauses between movements. A Western audience, however, tends to perceive these silences as a pointless void in which the throat may be noisily cleared. We must begin to exist in greater appreciation of these spaces and shadows. Another example of this might be traditional Chinese landscape painting, in which vast expanses of white parchment are left untouched, unpainted. To the artist, these negative spaces are deemed equally important and play an important role in balancing the composition, while providing areas of contemplative space for the onlooker to dwell within.

When regarded in this manner, space naturally takes on spiritual connotations. It becomes difficult to understand as it grates harshly against the Western model of progress and accountability, in which we must always be doing something and be able to represent our endeavours in a corporeal way. It takes supreme confidence and intelligence to not say and not do; yet this is frequently perceived as inertia and time wasting. To find beauty in nothingness and the tranquillity of negative space is a true gift. With increased familiarity and exposure, this lesson could begin to infect the consumer psyche, nurturing an appreciation of the art of not doing.

Foreignments, placebo realities and jolts

Change itself has a stimulating influence as it forces us to examine foreignments: to probe into the unknown in search of fresh information. Foreignments may be generated – or driven – provided the difference in a given network of meanings is only partially modified. Total difference will effectively place the network beyond perceivable recognition and, in so doing, will alienate users through an absence of lucid understanding and familiarity. As discussed in Chapter five when describing the work of Donald Norman, a 'just noticeable difference' (JND) is crucial if we are to develop relationships both incrementally and sustainably (see p113). This is, of course, how growth manifests itself, in steady micro-steps that only begin to show their presence through the passing of time. JNDs must be delivered and experienced by the user at a digestible rate in order to side step the trash-mongering onset of alienation. Periodically delivering a series of punctuated disruptions to the narrative provides an effective means of sustaining a connectedness between the subject and the object, and by doing so greatly increases the potential longevity of the relationship that follows.

JNDs are experienced by users as mild jolts – disruptive events – within an otherwise stable flow of information. They are fundamental ingredients of the jolt, as without incremental growth and sudden fluctuations in meaning, there can be no jolts. Film director David Lynch has developed a mastery over the delivery of such foreignments and their subsequent jolts, creating fake – or placebo – information flows that artfully fabricate credible portrayals of normalcy. Once crafted, Lynch proceeds to deconstruct this assembled sense of security. In *Blue Velvet*,[23] we find ourselves within a world that is so absolutely ordinary it is almost strange, a kind of proto-normality, if you will. However, all is not what it appears to be: this skilfully constructed placebo provides Lynch with the perfect foundation upon which to construct his jolts, and indeed he does. Although Lynch, like so many artists, has developed a compelling flair for the nurture of deception and mis-direction, the principles that he deploys are based simply on creating information flows and then suddenly shifting those flows at opportune moments.

Electronic products frequently portray a similarly deceptive guise; highly intelligent self-sufficiency is communicated by their lack of controls and minimal user interface, intended, undoubtedly, to increase the intensity of amazement when the product eventually does performs its wonders. This jolt forces us to question how something so simple is able to achieve so much. It is comparative in principle to minimalism, which has become an aesthetic genre in and of itself. An example of this can be found in the ironic arrogance put forward by the nouveau riche in their apparently spiritualized and uncluttered loft abodes, containing nothing but a bowl of dry rice and two smooth pebbles. In reality, a capitalist heart beats from behind the IKEA sliding panels and concealed attic storage hatch, where products hoarded in their multiples are sheepishly hidden from view.

This is, of course, a natural state of being for us humans and is no different from putting on your best shoes to go out on a Saturday night or, perhaps, checking your hair in the hall mirror before answering the door to sign for a parcel. It is practically a given that people show different sides to their personality depending upon to whom they are talking. We are subject to mood swings, and sometimes we just have off days where everything looks and feels wrong. All too often we see documentaries in which suburban residents utter, in deep shock, how seemingly normal the recently convicted serial killer from next door but one seemed. So frequently in daily life we are jolted in a manner similar to this and, subsequently, are required to reconstruct our assumptions and generalizations about the way in which things are in this complex and unstable world. These wake-up calls serve to remind us that things are seldom what they seem. This is perhaps one of the great strengths of the jolt and, certainly, where great design potential lies. Jolts challenge our preconceptions and, in so doing, wake us from the trance, encouraging us to re-evaluate and update our assumptions about a given thing. This is a vital sociological practice to engineer, as such regular acts of reappraisal ensure that our values and assumptions about the ever changing world continually update and adapt.

The ebb and flow of information that surges between subject and object is dramatically influenced by users themselves. We bring our own catalogue of meanings into any given network, and these meanings greatly influence the way in which the said network will be perceived. This means that no two people will perceive the same jolt – or PD – in the same way. The degree of self-projection that PDs allow, therefore, is influential to the extent that jolts are experienced as individual and self-reflective. By allowing the PDs to be experienced as personal, the jolts that result are, effectively, unique.

Mass-manufactured objects in possession of this degree of subject–object intimacy are, indeed rare, and have yet to find their way into the mainstream. That said, conceptual design proposals which endeavour to embed these values are of vital importance, as they serve to illustrate the potential for richer and, perhaps, more meaningful engagements with the made world. They also tend to point out through their own efficacy that so many jolts are, in fact, overcooked; products emerge from the shop floor so pregnant with meaning, so overloaded with prescribed values that they leave no room for the identity of the user. In so doing, products born of this mindset restrict themselves to a peripheral place in the hearts and minds of users, rather than the role of provocateur boldly situated at the forefront of user consciousness.

Chapter summary

Utopias are vital; they free us from the shackles of an imperfect present by revealing a limitless world of imaginable futures. Yet they also possess a dark side that sets up unrealistic expectations, generating false hopes and, ultimately, fostering restless cultures of perpetual disenchantment with the now.

. . . .

By producing streams of objects that signify Utopian values based upon a single prescribed and socially approved version of reality, material culture becomes inadvertently homogenized into one popular version.

. . . .

Fiction does not simply exist for the sole purpose of entertainment and is more than just a literary genre or category of movie *per se*. Fiction performs a vital role by weaving rich narrative threads throughout our daily lives.

. . . .

The desire to explore and consume fictions as perceived in objects bears strong similarities to the way in which we might consume a fictitious movie, play or novel; the emphasis is not on authenticity or truth, but on experience and meaning.

. . . .

As daily life continues to become more and more programmed, the need for fiction, complexity and dialogue in this over-streamlined world increases exponentially.

. . . .

New and, consequently, unfamiliar products radiate mysterious, enigmatic qualities that quickly crumble away once familiarity begins to accumulate between user and product.

· ·

For an object to continually portray a fictional *gestalt*, it must first possess an ability to conceal, holding a few cards up its sleeve in order to avoid total discovery.

· ·

Products possessing overly programmed semantics, or *perfect* products, are particularly vulnerable to the glare of de-fictioning; they are too easy to map and pigeonhole.

· ·

Deeper and more intense bonds are forged between users and objects when products portray a perceivable sense of consciousness. This is not to say that objects should literally be conscious; but, rather, a given object may react to its surroundings with an ontological receptiveness and flexibility of judgement that creates the impression of – or simulates – consciousness.

· ·

Tools that begin to explore consciousness simulation, such as artificial intelligence and artificial life, are all too frequently discussed in terms of their ability to remove the decision-making process from humans.

· ·

We bring our own psychological baggage into the meaning-consumption loop; this is why material engagements can seem so personal to us.

· ·

We pick up brief reflections of identity through phantile drives (PDs) buried deep within products' layers of signification. PDs are like motors that generate meaning once perceived; they are phantile in the sense that they are both metaphysical and deeply suggestive.

· ·

PDs are frequently deployed to generate eye-opening jolts and quirky surprises, like the hello greeting on a HIFI display. Gimmicks such as these exemplify one way of working with PDs. They deliver an opening jolt of reasonable intensity, yet somehow fail to sustain wonderment through the passing of time, due once again to the PDs' inability to grow and evolve over time.

· ·

The designing of omnipresent PDs may be facilitated by incorporating a measure of openness – or space – within product semantics, enhancing the degree of self that may be invested into the discursive engagement between subject and object.

· ·

Foreignments may be generated or driven, provided that the difference in a given network of meanings is only partially modified. Total difference will effectively place the network beyond perceivable recognition and, in so doing, will alienate the user through an absence of lucid understanding and familiarity.

· ·

The ebb and flow of information that surges between subject and object is dramatically influenced by users themselves. We bring our own catalogue of meanings into any given network, and these meanings greatly influence the way in which the said network will be perceived. This means that no two people will perceive the same jolt – or PD – in the same way.

· ·

PDs deliver surprises and jolts. Omnipresent PDs render the said surprises and jolts amorphous, enabling them to evolve through time while the user simultaneously evolves and grows.

A toolbox of ideas

Experience over authenticity: when embedding fictions within the semantic layers of an object, try to focus on their experiential dimensions rather than what simply constitutes conventional reality *per se*. Thinking beyond – or simply ignoring – the accountable will unveil a far greater potential. We should not be inhibited by inept notions of accountability and truth; instead, let us explore the profound and the numinous in search of alternative and more provocative modes of material engagement.

· ·

Avoid cheap tricks: PDs are, indeed, potent meaning generators, but only when they are deployed in a subtle and artful manner. To achieve and sustain this level of sensitivity, it may sometimes be necessary for the driven meaning to appear accidental, engendering further meaning within the user while reducing the gap between subject and object. PDs must not be signposted; they should be unwittingly discovered by the user.

· ·

Keep it moving: it is crucial that fictions evolve and grow; if they are static – providing one single repetitive jolt – they will soon lose their impact and subsequently become de-fictioned by the user. To remain potent, therefore, fiction must continually enchant users by shifting and evolving at all times. Transience of this kind may be achieved through deliberately deceiving or misdirecting users, creating multiple false information flows that may be switched at any time.

. . . .

Avoid over-programming: it is vital that a degree of ambiguity and space is embedded within a given product semantic. This means that although sufficient intuitive information may be made evident for the user to operate the product, undefined interactive space should also be made available to be explored and defined by the subject as the relationship unfolds. This undefined space also provides a kind of mirror, which reflects back the individual idiosyncrasies of each user, rendering each interaction unique and personal.

chapter seven

real world feasibility

The vision

Imagine a world in which humans and objects coexist, living out epic tales of adoration, love and, above all, empathy – a sensual realm wherein the walls erected to separate flesh from polymer crumble giving way to a lawless and unsupervised consumer future. The born and the made – people and things – develop a oneness that finally enables them to coexist over vast periods of time in complete symbiosis. Imagine a world in which products are designed to support the investment of emotion – cherishable products, appliances and tools that not only sustain but also amplify sensations of attachment – a world where technological modernity is not the sole value indicator and Personal Digital Assistants (PDAs), laptops and MP3s (a computer file format that stores a large amount of information in a small amount of space – usually music) may triumphantly bear the scars of age. This is a consumable future that abounds with penetrative sensations of mutuality, where potent emotional attachments proliferate and definitions between subject and object become blurred. Imagine a world in which the new economic system does not equate quality of life with quantity of production, but where successful partnerships, degrees of empathy and sustained emotional attachments are the new performance indicators – a world of symbiosis situated far beyond the hegemonic dominion of master and slave so painstakingly fostered by the old capitalist system. Finally, imagine a world with less waste, minimized pollution and reduced resource depletion where economic interests prosper and consumers may satisfy their fleeting desires without causing further devastation to this fragile planet.

The real world

The real world is a short-sighted place of which, 'ideas people', are habitually reminded of by those in favour of the blanket-like familiarity of a superficially understood world. The real world is a term that precedes a put-down usually attempting to jam new ideas for fear of them disrupting the flow of a superficially understood world. Creative thinkers and full-time dreamers alike are commonly reminded of their absence from the real world, as though their life up to that point had existed within some metaphysical dream, or that it might be possible for two people to work in the same office but simultaneously exist in two different worlds, one of them real the other not. Although the real world serves to prompt justification of how new ideas might be successfully integrated within current working practices, it invariably behaves as an impervious obstruction to both change and progress, in an age where change and progress are absolutely vital to our future survival. There is also a monetary agenda. Developed world societies tend to measure success with wealth; thus, the real world will only value sustainable design strategies when they support economic growth. Sadly, the real world will always be a place with economic accountability as its key entry requirement.

A formal discussion on what constitutes reality would normally follow at this point. However, in truth, we each occupy our own world, our own handcrafted version of reality in which all makes perfect sense – to us anyway. Concepts of reality are described here as being *handcrafted* by the self; upon cognition, each of us filters information about the world based on our prior knowledge of it. Memory is also used to further modify the information we hold in order to craft an ever more distorted interpretation of actual reality:

> The senses do not provide access to absolute truth. Experiences only take on meaning through personal memories, personal belief structures and personal choices. My environment is not what I see, hear, feel, smell or taste. And even then, I am the one who gives meaning to it all. I am the scriptwriter of my world. I give reason and meaning to that world and everything that happens within it. In giving that meaning, I create my world.[1]

Meaning is not something self-sufficient that lurks dormant within the semantic layers of an object until someone accidentally notices it, nor can it be universally designed or programmed. Meanings are created between people and things, and though designers can endeavour to create and trigger meaningful sensations within users, the explicit nature of those meanings is largely beyond the designers' control. This is because users will contort, bend and modify meaning until it fits neatly into their own construct of reality; meanings are unconsciously customized by each user in their own particular way to create bespoke renderings of a formerly mass-produced meaning. It may therefore be said that 'the only difference between designer and user is that the designer has made a career of creating meaning'.[2] Designers trigger meaning by presenting users with provocative scenarios from which meaning may be unconsciously recognized and extracted through cognitive engagement. These meanings will then be contorted – bent out of all proportion – until crafted to a point where they accurately support the user's perception of self.

For example, when two individual people and their respective worlds collide, anomalies are quickly identified that can either be embraced as inspiring and new, or rejected as misguided, incompatible and obtuse. Normally, the latter prevails as we generally seek companionship from like-minded individuals whose presence in our lives serves to reinforce our own fragile concept of how things really work in the world. This is why groups of friends are often seen in cafés, slow-nodding their way through one another's anecdotes, to show that they both understand and empathize with the words and experiences of the other person. Cynical as it may sound, friends are unwittingly hand picked in this way, as their reassurance and empathetic support is what we really crave. When self-reflective similarities are recognized in others, two previously isolated worlds collide, each world serving to reinforce – and often contribute to – the other, which in turn manifests a lasting degree of empathy between the two people. In this way, friendships are born and strong empathic unions are forged between two previously isolated entities. Analogies may be drawn here to material consumption: the acquisition of self-reflective artefacts is largely motivated by the same human search for empathy and the external reinforcement of one's individual identity as being separate from society. We seek a similar degree of existential reinforcement from the things we own as we do from the people we choose to be around.

In the broadest of terms, the real world is designated simply through popularity; it is what most people opt for and anyone who disagrees – or, perhaps, sees things in a slightly different way – is clearly not living in the real world anymore. This is, of course, a fundamentally flawed premise, as popularity alone does not necessarily signify a degree of quality or any lasting truth. If that were the case, then the Spice Girls would still be topping the charts and McDonald's would be at the forefront of everyone's eating agenda. Therefore, it can be recognized that the real world is a transient and singular concept that assumes only one correct approach and an infinite number of incorrect ones – a grossly inept model, indeed, when all that is needed is a pluralism of equally valued and constantly evolving viewpoints that generate provocative yet worthwhile debate surrounding the way in which we design the future. Sustainable design is not a set of neatly arranged and predefined formulas or legislation-driven principles, but a critical and provocative debate surrounding the way in which we intend to live with this fragile Earth. It is from debate of this nature that radical new ideas are born and positive future change is stimulated.

An outdated model

In a world that is ever changing, inert strategic and theoretical models quickly become anti-evolutionary and grossly counterproductive. It is shocking, then, to recognize that 'the current model of capitalism is based on a pre-industrial revolution worldview dating back almost 200 years, in which the quantity of production equates to the quality of human life'.[3] The prevailing view was then – and still is today – that the more we produce and sell, the stronger the economy becomes and, ultimately, the higher the standard of living that can be expected. Logical as it may at first appear, a rapidly deteriorating biosphere disproves the accuracy of this equation simply by placing the future of human life itself in the balance:

> When we objectively view the recent past – and 200 years is recent even in terms of human evolution and certainly in terms of biological evolution – one fact becomes clear: the industrial revolution as we now know it is not sustainable. We cannot keep using materials and resources the way we do now.[4]

Back in the earlier days of the industrial revolution, environmental awareness was minimal, to say the least, and the idea that certain natural resources were finite was practically unheard of, so the factories with their new and efficient machinery spat out unsurpassed volumes of product to the wonder and amazement of all. Production was uninhibited and raged forth to pioneer a seemingly flawless economic model, a model that would soon outlive the planet's ability to support it.

Although the way in which we conduct business today has evolved practically beyond recognition, the capitalist system that underpins the majority of corporate affairs has changed very little – stoically persisting that the measure of manufacturing output somehow equates to that of societal well-being, and that a booming economy serves to testify that all is well in this part of the world. It is therefore particularly ironic that this same system currently regards the environmental fall-out of production and consumption – such as toxic waste, dwindling natural resources and global warming – as secondary issues of relative unimportance; surely these issues are equally relevant, if not more so? The underlying premise of sustainable development can be distinguished as a societal process in which ecological limits are both recognized and respected. It is quite clear that current economic practices do not do this; so to what extent can we claim to be pursuing sustainable development when the economic system upon which all commercial activity is founded remains largely blind to it?

Having a fluent economy that affords ceaseless developed world creature comforts, while commanding that familiar measure of global authoritarianism that we have become so accustomed to in the developed North, is important to many. After all, economic affluence is not necessarily a bad thing in and of itself; however, it does come with a need for greater ethical awareness and ecological responsibility. The world's handful of economic superpowers consumes far more than its share of natural resources, transformed through the process of production and consumption into vast quantities of waste. This waste is a critical problem not only in terms of space and where to put it; but more terminally, it is symptomatic of a characteristic pattern of inefficient consumption found in the majority of affluent capitalist societies. The excessive consumption of the US, for example, has a catastrophic impact on the planet as a whole. With approximately 4.7 per cent of the world's population, it manages to consume nearly a quarter of the world's resources, while the industrialized world takes a massive 80 per cent share of the natural resources consumed today, to supply a mere 20 per cent of the world's population. Needless to say, economic dominance comes at a high price to the natural world, though at present this price is given little consideration and barely registers on the economic radar.

Of course, things are slowly changing and have been for several years now. A number of large corporations are beginning to see their responsibilities running throughout the entire product life cycle, and many have set competitive goals for enhancing the sustainability of their operations over the coming years. Whether these changes are motivated by a genuine concern for ecological preservation, or simply to accommodate forthcoming environmental legislation remains to be seen. Perhaps their motivation should not be of concern: the important thing is that attitudes are slowly beginning to change and this can only be beneficial in the long term. Economic success and environmental sustainability can no longer be dealt with in isolation since environmental factors are an intrinsic facet of economic survival in the modern world. Environmental sensitivity is becoming an increasingly cost-effective practice for today's future-facing corporations, both in terms of avoiding legislation breach, such as increasingly demanding take-back or reclamation policies and landfill

Figure 7.1

Waste could be seen as a symptom of a failed relationship

Source: Photograph by Katherine Anne Rose © 2005

taxation, but perhaps more so by generating capital via the creation of sustainable brand values and the positive associations that they foster within increasingly environmentally aware consumers.

When considering the future extension of product lifespan, the underlying question might still, however, be: *how can the company survive if we only sell one unit per consumer?* This would seem, at first, to be a valid question. To suggest that consumers should keep what they have – and for longer – grates harshly against the current model of Western capitalism. Yet, in allowing consumers to develop a degree of empathy with the products they own, you automatically nurture a visceral empathy with that particular brand. The felt sense of empathy resonates deeply within consumers' perceptions of a particular corporation's core values, and this is vigorously influential over both the intensity and longevity of relationships that consumers establish with a particular brand. It can therefore be seen that in terms of sustainability, the efficacy of conventional capitalism must be questioned; more lucrative models must surely exist than the blind nurturing of endless sequences of desire and destruction that are the hallmarks of Western capitalism today.

Sustainable design is unresolved

Sustainable design is a relatively new arrival on the creative scene with a great deal still to learn. For this reason alone, it must remain open to new possibilities. After all, it is quite possible that the methods through which we currently address sustainability are not as sustainable as we might like to think. As a specialized approach, sustainable design takes the wider creative industries several steps closer to an environmentally benign future. Yet, despite the future conscious ethos of this new and ambitious design movement, there appears to be a distinct lack of innovation surrounding its below-the-line strategic methodologies. Perhaps due to the discipline's youth, present approaches seem to lack philosophical depth. It could be argued that in their current guise, the majority of methods deployed by sustainable designers today do not actually attend to the root causes of the problems we face, instead focusing almost primarily on solutions that attend to the after-effects – or symptoms – of our wasteful and grossly inefficient existence. The end result is that consumers continue wastefully forth, only now they do so with recycled materials instead of virgin ones. A dangerously liberated conscience also results, which frequently serves to stimulate even greater degrees of wasteful consumption.

Many practitioners in the field of sustainable design will be familiar with the *three Rs* principle: *reduce, re-use* and *recycle.* The original contribution made by this uncomplicated trichotomy was, firstly, to state that our top priority should be to simply reduce consumption; that means making less, buying less, using less, etc. Secondly, we were asked to re-use all that we could to avoid wasting materials and, of course, stimulating the need for further manufacturing of replacement goods. Third, and finally, we were asked to recycle, but only when the previous two options of reducing and re-using were unattainable. During recent years, this golden principle has pretty much gone out the window: recycling has been boldly promoted to the number one slot, while its relegated counterparts – reduce and re-use – are now seldom discussed, let alone implemented.

Governmental legislation often serves to drive recycling initiatives, rather than re-use or reduction strategies, as recycling is more immediately compatible with economic growth in its current form. In addition, recycling is a commercial activity in itself, paying the wages of a fast-growing national workforce while making an equally fast-growing contribution to the national economy. Although alignment with commercial and economic systems is a relevant consideration, it must certainly be questioned as to whether it is wise to give recycling the prominence that it currently enjoys. As discussed earlier in this book, recycling is not a one-stop solution to sustainable production and consumption, and it is essential that consumers are not misled into believing that it is.

In addition to a predominately symptom-focused approach, sustainable design also possesses a slightly anthropocentric persona that occasionally obstructs progress by serving the interests of human activity before that of the biosphere. In instances such as these, it must be questioned as to whether we are actually sustaining the environment or just its economic viability. The recycling of plastics, for example, is largely motivated by a concern for the diminishing natural resource: oil. We have been educated to believe that when the planet's reserves of oil dry up – as they eventually will – ecological tragedy awaits us; but does it really? A true friend of the Earth might argue that the end of naturally occurring oil will bring a similar end to the petrol-guzzling motor car since without oil there can be no petrol, forcing us to develop alternative means of locomotion, such as hydrogen-powered cars. This certainly does not mean that recycling is a counterproductive endeavour, or even that we should abandon recycling and become as wasteful as possible in order to hurriedly bring about the aforementioned changes. Rather, sustainability is a complex issue in need of constant reappraisal. If the focus of this debate were to switch materials from plastic to wood, for example, recycling would suddenly become a matter of paramount importance.

We are all familiar with the devastating impacts of deforestation, and any design strategy that reduces the unsustainable felling of trees must be supported wholeheartedly. Apart from the rich array of biodiversity they support, trees make up a large percentage of the planet's natural air filtration system, and so without them we have a problem. The consumption of paper and card also contributes massively to deforestation, and effective recycling initiatives in this material area alone make a dramatic contribution. It may be stated, therefore, that although recycling is anything but a one-stop solution to sustainable production and consumption, it does make one single great stride in the right direction, taking us a little closer to an efficient and *more* sustainable future. It is also worth noting that the recent shift in public attitude that makes recycling possible is considerable. This public readiness to embrace sustainability can only be seen as encouraging for sustainable designers as it indicates both a societal sympathy for ecological issues, along with a participatory willingness to get involved and éxplore new means of material engagement.

The way in which we both discuss and name our practice also needs resolving, and fast. Large amounts of time and energy are spent attempting to define whether what you do is design for environment, eco-design, sustainable design, design for sustainability, low-impact design, green design, clean design, and so on, and so on. As with most things, this is a matter of opinion; but does it really matter what we call it? Of course, some terms are more helpful than others. Clean design is attractive to industry because it shrugs off the baggage that seems to accompany words such as 'green' and 'eco' – the very sounds of which conjure lucid visions of an ascetic lifestyle or a barren existence defined by sacrificial non-enjoyment. Many practitioners are beginning to believe that there should be no such thing as sustainable design, claiming that it is wrong to departmentalize environmentally aware design practice as it should simply be integrated within conventional design practice without ceremony. Essentially, catering for the needs of the natural environment is simply another element of good design.

The word *sustainability* may be too vast to be of any real value; it is an umbrella term that attempts to encompass all activities geared toward reducing the negative social and environmental impacts of contemporary life. In real terms, for a system to be classified as being truly sustainable it must possess the ability to be maintained indefinitely and must be capable of continuation *ad infinitum*. Due largely to entropy, none of our current strategies even closely align with this description; energy is always lost somewhere in the loop. Furthermore, the term sustainability wrongfully implies that we should nurture the planet, just as a gardener tends their plot. It may actually be counterproductive to see our role on Earth in this way, as the Earth does not belong to us, nor does it need nursing like some sick puppy. It just wants to be left well alone so that it can get on with the slow and arduous task of replenishing itself. We are simply just another species living on this Earth, and it seems obvious that an end to our days will eventually come. In the vast timeline stretching from the moment of creation – known as the *big bang* – to the present day, the human species is but a mere pin prick, nothing more than a blip.

In some ways, heroically attempting to *save the environment* is like breaking someone's leg and then offering them a lift to the hospital. We caused the damage, and though we should, indeed, be doing all we can to put it right, there is absolutely nothing noble or righteous about it. It is time to stop regarding sustainable design as some kind of ethical crusade or a self-sacrificial gesture. Essentially, sustainability is a long-term journey that aims to seek out more efficient methods for us to live on this planet, and serves to meet social, economic and environmental interests. Yes, recycling waste makes a valid contribution to the preservation of resources, while reducing waste; but we could potentially be doing so much more. Sustainable design should not simply be a question of recycling, disassembling unwanted products and designing biodegradable waste; the potential is far greater than this. Approaches such as these are wholly symptom focused and sorely neglect the actual root cause of the environmental problem we currently face. We must not be lulled into a false sense of security simply because we now have these methodologies, closing the book and essentially bringing the sustainable design debate to a close before it has even begun to gather momentum.

Strategic countermeasures to our wasteful and grossly inefficient model of production and consumption, such as design for disassembly, design for recycling, and the specification of recyclable and biodegradable materials, are already in place and have been so for a number of years – most of which attempt to address the after-effects of our wasteful production and consumption cycles. Despite the apparent future-conscious ethos of these countermeasures, they attend to symptoms rather than causes. We must develop an understanding of the actual drivers that underpin our wasteful consumption crisis if anything like an ecologically sustainable design culture is to develop. In reality, the sustainability debate has only just begun, and this is exactly why new and provocative genres of sustainable design must constantly be explored, so that this ongoing debate about how best to live in greater harmony with the world may continue to grow both in its philosophical diversity and long-term efficacy.

Despite the complexity and numerous hypocrisies which underpin sustainability, one thing is certain: a sustainable design culture that practices more than just recycling, energy efficiency and design for disassembly must be nurtured. Well-intentioned approaches such as these should be seen as essential components of efficient production and consumption, and be practised universally regardless of any environmental claims or ethical righteousness. As a creative discipline, sustainable design is most certainly unresolved and must continue to delve deeper still to the very root of human consciousness, as this is exactly where both the problems and the solutions lie to what is essentially a human-made environmental crisis.

The cost of environmental unawareness

The halcyon days when large corporations were in a position to choose whether to jump on the sustainability bandwagon or not are finally coming to an end. Sustainability is a mounting imperative, and one that will only continue to grow over the years to come. In terms of sustainability, an industry-wide shift in attitude has been steadily gathering pace over the past few decades; this attitude shift may, of course, be attributed to the awakening ecological consciousness of society as a whole. In this way, industry is essentially updating its practices in order to comply with the changing demands of the consumer. At present, the majority of large corporations make changes only when they have to, as business attitudes are predominately legislation driven. One of the major factors that has brought about today's commercial interest in environmental issues has simply been the ensuing barrage of legislation that currently makes its way towards businesses in the European Union. Pressure is imposed on industry by the legislative demands of an increasingly concerned government. It may be said that, in most cases, industry has pulled its socks up simply to avoid being penalized financially for violating environmental law.

Legislation is a crucial component in bringing about necessary changes in commercial attitude, though it must be said that legislation itself seldom attends to consumer-side issues. It is primarily industry focused, and is somewhat neglectful of the pivotal role played by users in the quest for a more sustainable future. Legislative policies generally serve as 'very broad, non-prescriptive policy tools that push the industrial system in the desired direction, without trying to define the end-point, either organizationally or technologically'.[5] They also tend to leave design out of the loop by adopting the role of watchdog to industry, policing the sustainability of industrial processes rather than that of the entire cycle consisting of design, manufacture, consumption and waste. Nevertheless, mounting legislation continually turns up the heat on industry and never more so than today; the resulting pressure on industry to be ecologically accountable is increasing fast. Manufacturers, in particular, face great financial loss by being ill prepared for ensuing legislation, both in terms of the asset-crippling fines that result from failing to meet new standards and, perhaps more crucially, by making way for competitors in both domestic and export markets whose products have greater environmental appeal. It is therefore imperative that we – as a creative industry – pioneer new ways of working in compliance with forthcoming legislative demands: ways which empower industry to act with the degree of freedom that it has become so accustomed to, while avoiding the costly breach of environmental legislation. Without adequate preparation, companies will find themselves desperately struggling to keep up with the changes that will soon be upon them; as a result, huge financial penalties resulting from the breach of new environmental legislation will swiftly bring about their economic collapse.

As discussed earlier, today's prevailing industrial model has a tendency to perceive production as a linear process of resource extraction, manufacture and sales, with little or no consideration given to events that occur afterwards. It may also be said that product life is currently of little concern to the majority of industrialists, provided that when the time does come to replace the product, customers come back and brand loyalty is sustained. However, times are changing, and consumers are becoming increasingly aware of both the social, environmental and personal implications of their purchasing decisions. Recent research has shown that a massive 75 per cent of consumers claim to favour products with tangible environmental advantages and would invariably choose these over competitive products. 'Three-quarters of the people polled in the UK say that they would make a choice of products on a green or ethical basis, and 28 per cent say that they actually have chosen or boycotted a product or company for ethical reasons over the past 12 months.'[6] These dramatic figures indicate that the future survival of many large brands will become increasingly dependent upon both the delivery and perceptibility of environmentally conscious practices and products. Positive and lasting associations with a given brand can be forged in this way, and these associations are intensely influential over the buying decisions of most consumers. 'Eighty-six per cent of British consumers say they have a more positive image of a company if they see it doing something to make the world a better place.'[7] Furthermore:

> A survey by Gallup found that nine out of ten consumers would make a special effort to buy products from companies trying to protect the environment. Surveys by Nielsen and at Oxford University found that two-thirds of consumers say that they would pay more for products with environmental benefits.[8]

A number of forward-facing corporations have begun to grasp this concept, and to surprisingly successful ends. Already ahead of a number of its corporate rivals, domestic electronics giant Sony adopts a highly competitive environmental stance, particularly when it comes to new product innovation, packaging and energy efficiency. For example, Sony recently achieved less than 1 watt standby power consumption for a large share of its products, Sony camcorders now use completely lead-free solders and all Sony packaging now deploys recycling technologies to ensure the optimal balance between material consumption and product protection. Sony also has a number of product recycling initiatives in operation throughout the world, along with an exciting new refurbishment programme that aims to extend the life of some higher-volume goods, such as Discmans, Walkmans, PlayStations and mobile phones. It can therefore be said that Sony is definitely doing its bit for the environment; however, when faced with such a receptive consumer marketplace, could it actually be doing more?

The majority of consumers would not initially associate Sony with sustainability, as most consumers are largely oblivious of the great length that Sony is actually going to. Of course, Sony made a conscious decision to keep quiet about their environmental agenda, choosing instead to discuss it within a fairly dry and *de rigueur* environmental report that can be found buried within the depths of their vast corporate website. This approach to sustainability is not exclusive to Sony; numerous other corporations of a similar size and stature go to considerable lengths to continually revise the sustainability of their operations, yet few consumers will ever hear of it. It is commonly assumed that talk of sustainability will induce a sensation of compromise within potential consumers, particularly within the digital product genre where all is supposed to be shiny and new. However, ample evidence exists to clearly indicate otherwise.

Sustainable design – and the broader issue of sustainability as a whole – must cease to be regarded as a whimsical marketing strategy or some value-adding after thought. Environmental sensitivity is the very foundation that must underpin any corporate visioning in an increasingly ecologically aware marketplace. It can reinforce brand values while empowering companies to act freely without continual bombardment from asset-crippling fines resulting from legislative breach, which are usually followed by an image-bruising aftershock of negative press. Times are changing, and significant conceptual shifts are greatly needed in the way in which we regard environmentally aware business practice. We now know that sustainability is compatible with economic growth and we should begin to push this notion forward with far greater confidence. Clearly, the very concept of sustainability has accumulated more than its fair share of baggage over the past few decades and comes loaded with preconception. Despite this, we must persist in driving the debate forth, and pioneer new ways to sustain both the economy and the deteriorating natural environment upon which it so precariously rests.

Consumers have a more positive image of a company if they see it doing something to make the world a better place. There are numerous indications that environmental considerations percolate through finished products into the consumer psyche, creating positive brand associations. It may therefore be said that brand loyalty is facilitated, in part, by a corporation's ability to clearly communicate sustainable brand values through the delivery of environmentally conscious products and services. When engaging with products of this nature, consumers feel that they are investing in a good cause and their consumption is, in some way, helping to make the world a better place. In direct contrast to this, loyalty to a particular brand is also threatened when large corporations neglect and abuse their environmental responsibilities. The damage caused by this behaviour is beyond measure, as it comes with a substantial aftershock of negative brand associations that lingers in the consumer psyche for an eternity. These lasting negative associations can be so potent that consumers may cease to invest in certain branded products or services, and switch to a competitor's brand in search of a new relationship. Not only have loyal customers been driven away, weakening the company, they have gone to the competitor, strengthening the other side. Market share is lost and a firm monetary body-blow is dealt from which it will take some time to recover. When one considers the vast sums of money that large corporations invest per annum in marketing, public relations (PR), advertising and a host of other edge-giving services to engender positive brand values, it becomes a remarkable oversight for the same corporation to demolish these painstakingly constructed values in a single environmental blunder. If for no other reason than to sustain market share, it is of critical importance that the decision-makers of large corporations begin to recognize the impact that their environmental agendas have within the hearts and minds of the consumers who, essentially, keep them in business. Sustainability affects us all, regardless of our ethics or political stance on the environment.

The steady increase in legislation such as product take-back policies and landfill taxation is already beginning to engage designers in re-evaluating the importance of product life consideration. At present, products designed for take-back are generally geared toward economical disassembly and recycling/re-use, but can still come at a cost to producers. As a result of this legislation, waste generated by the current model of consumption will soon render it an economically detrimental practice. Failure to accommodate the demands of environmental legislation in future concepts will incur added costs, making the legislation a dangerous thing to ignore. Indeed, legislation will come and go and will naturally evolve and change over time, as with all things political. Yet although the nature and focus of environmental legislation will change over time, the fact remains that legislation will always exist, and therefore designers need to begin acknowledging it as a relevant design criteria in the ever more sustainable marketplace of the future.

Though a major step in the right direction, complying with legislation alone is simply not enough; designers must pioneer new ways of working in compliance with increasing legislative demands without compromising creativity or commercial edge. It is commonly perceived that embracing environmental factors is to compromise, or to do without. The way in which sustainability is perceived must, therefore, adapt from the sacrificial low-tech, beige and crusty world it currently inhabits, to a multi-tech discipline of radically new and provocative creative opportunities – a chance to start over and conduct an industry-wide reappraisal of material culture. Sustainability provides us with the greatest opportunity to radically rethink the way in which we engage with our material worlds. Legislation provides the guidance and a persuasive schedule within which these changes need to be implemented, while giving us the gentle shove that we need to get started.

Producer and consumer

Times are slowly beginning to change, and the once reckless manner in which our material empires were fabricated now treads a new and ambitious path toward a cleaner and more efficient future. We are all aware of the efforts expended annually on recycling, design which facilitates ease of disassembly, and great enhancements in the energy efficiency of electronic objects. One of the most revolutionary transformations that is currently emerging is simply a shift in emphasis of the relationships that are established between consumers and producers. Facile as it may at first sound, this minor systemic adaptation may well provide the greatest ecological offering of all as it looks beyond the symptoms of our problem, and taps directly into the root of our looming environmental crisis to address the wasteful transience of contemporary material consumption.

It was once the case that consumers were practically forgotten about post-purchase, each one being regarded on a boardroom level as just another punter, another unit sold. Thankfully, times are changing and in the sustainable marketplace of the future, selling a product and then forgetting about the customer will constitute an uneconomical and desperately short-term practice. We already know that by formulating a commercial system that enables consumers to develop empathy with the products they own, you also enable a visceral loyalty with that particular brand. Products then become talking points, linking consumers to producers though ongoing dialogues regarding the families of products that unite them – remodelling corporate culture away from a temporal world of one-off sales toward a reflexive domain of relationship management which symbolizes a 'fundamental change in the relationship between producer and consumer, a shift from an economy of goods and purchases to one of service and flow'.[9] This remodelling can be likened to both Walter Stahel's and Michael Braungart's vision of a 'service economy'[10], where consumers lease products rather than buy them.

The leasing and sharing of products is on the rise, though generally motivated through convenience and affordability rather than through any great environmental agenda. Despite this, the leasing of products has distinct advantages over the conventional system of conspicuous consumption characterized so neatly by a cyclic monologue of serial buying and discarding. In the leasing model, consumers can regularly exchange and upgrade their appliances at a moment's notice in order to ensure that they always have the latest models. The cost of servicing and repair is discreetly written into the monthly rental fee, making it perceivably free, which in itself strips away the anxiety from owning costly and, ultimately, breakable artefacts. For the majority of consumers, the overall cost of leasing is relatively affordable, too, making it a particularly competitive option. Leased products are also attractive from an environmental perspective, as they are always returned to the store once users are ready to upgrade, which immediately renders the process of recycling far more cost effective. It is also common for leased objects to serve more than one user, and a leased DVD player, for example, may have two or three different owners in a single lifetime, while a less technologically transient product, such as a washing machine, may touch the lives of over five families during a single lifetime. When given the enormous benefits of leasing over buying, it becomes particularly odd that leasing still remains such an unpopular option.

Consumers deploy objects to designate their particular being as separate from that of society, and the process of owning objects and engaging with material culture enables this vital self-defining process to occur. It appears that despite obvious advantages, leasing encounters a fundamental problem due to the psychological nature of ownership, and the innate need within each of us to actually own things and designate them as ours. Consumers tend to feel that objects do not actually belong to them if they are not at liberty to throw them away the moment they feel the need to do so. In addition to this, asking consumers to essentially borrow their products, and compromise the diversity and wealth of their otherwise owned material empires, is an ambitious aim. 'Owning tangible things is an undeniable human need. Products provide symbols of identity to their users and the people around them. They carry meaning and are constant reminders of who we are, where we are, our activities, our history and our future.'[11] Objects also behave as powerful memory cues and:

> … can remind us of our past achievements, relationships, etc, and become
> concrete manifestations of our personal biography. In other words, they can

become extensions of our self. Functioning as our external memories, they assure us of the persistence of our identity and integrity of our being over time. Accordingly we develop strong emotional attachment to some objects because they played some part in memorable events of our past.[12]

Due to the current conflicts of leasing with the enduring human need for the absolute ownership of things, the bright sentiments of leasing as a contemporary industrial model might better be expressed through product life extension, upgrade and maintenance – in short, a deeper after-sales relationship between producer and consumer that essentially enables the absolute ownership of longer-lasting things.

In the winter of 1996/1997, the Eternally Yours Foundation – a group active in the field of product life research – organized three meetings to discuss different aspects of product lifespan. One of these, entitled *Sales 'n' Service*, revealed that a large number of companies are moving away from just selling products, toward both fostering and maintaining relationships with their customers. Their findings indicated that 'in sustaining relations, the material product mainly serves as a conversation piece that keeps on generating turnover for years after its birth'.[13] Eternally Yours refer to this period as a *use career*, and consider this period of engagement between subject and object as the greatest means for businesses to generate further turnover, while also reducing the unnecessary volumes of production and consumption that have become so characteristic of the modern world. Turnover can still be generated long after an item has been sold, and for this reason we should cease to recoil in terror at the very thought of extending product life. On the contrary, if revenue can be generated long after a product has been sold – without the need, for example, for further costly manufacturing, resource extraction, energy consumption, atmospheric pollution and waste – it can only be regarded as a more lucrative destiny for corporate visionaries to pursue. 'There are trends in the current economy which point to a "decoupling" of economic activities from its physical metabolism.'[14] Designers and manufacturers, therefore, should begin to see their responsibilities as spanning the whole period of time that the product is being used, shifting their focus onto maintenance, upgrade and after-sales service, rather than just once at the moment of transaction in the store:

The supreme moment of transfer should not be the finale of development processes, but just the first stage. So, besides reckoning with discarding and recycling, product design includes setting up or adapting relevant services: cleaning, repairing, upgrading, transport, spare parts, information desks and, in some cases, even facilities to support shared use.[15]

The notion of a use career is helpful in reframing the way in which we approach the design and production of objects, as it takes into account the whole life cycle of objects, defining their lifespan in terms of use rather than material or component longevity. This term also incorporates the idea of a career, which is a developmental process of continual incremental growth. By developing deeper relationships with their customers, companies empower themselves by being able to continuously predict and cater for their customers' changing and growing needs. This also has deep impacts upon the consumer's perception of a particular corporation's core values and the subsequent relationships that they develop with specific brands. Products serve as conversation pieces – connecting producers with consumers – to provide a timely migration away from the temporal world of one-off sales toward a reflexive and sustainable domain of relationship management, service and flow.

What is being proposed is a partial shift in business strategy to acheive this migration. The result is a corporation that sustains market share by adapting to an increasingly sustainable marketplace in an efficient and perceivably forward-facing manner – challenging corporate, academic and professional worldviews to shape the future in a responsible, humanistic and meaningful way.

As always, design will play a pivotal role here: for this system to be effective, consumers must first possess the desire to hold onto their products for greater lengths of time. It is all well and good for strategists, futurologists and environmentalists to propound theories of longevity and elongated consumption cycles; but if end users have no desire to keep things for longer, ultimately, they will not. We therefore need to design products that consumers will actually want to keep, maintain and use for longer periods of time, sustaining their value to keep users caught in the hook of consuming them. Such objects are designed for empathy and are created in an artful way, engendering powerful emotional attachments, rich evolving narratives, intense user experience and a sustained element of uncertainty and fiction.

Chapter summary

Although the way in which we conduct business today has evolved beyond recognition, the capitalist system that underpins modern corporate affairs has changed very little, persisting that the measure of output from production and manufacturing equates that of societal well-being.

· ·

Environmental sensitivity is becoming an increasingly cost-effective practice for future-facing corporations, both in terms of avoiding legislation breach and generating capital via the creation of sustainable brand values.

· ·

In allowing consumers to develop a degree of empathy with the products they own, you automatically nurture a visceral empathy with that particular brand.

· ·

In terms of sustainability, the efficacy of conventional capitalism must be questioned; more lucrative models exist than the blind nurturing of endless sequences of desire and destruction.

· ·

The methods through which we currently address sustainability may not be as sustainable as we think.

· ·

Environmentally-aware consumers continue wastefully forth, only now they do so with recycled materials instead of virgin ones. Although it makes a noteworthy stride in the right direction, recycling is not a one-stop solution to sustainable production and consumption.

· ·

Sustainability has us nurturing the planet. The Earth does not belong to us, nor does it need nursing like some sick puppy; it just wants to be left well alone.

· ·

Sustainable design must delve deeper still to the root of human consciousness, as this is where the solutions lie to what is a human-made environmental crisis.

· ·

One of the major factors that has brought about today's commercial interest in environmental issues has been the ensuing barrage of legislation that currently makes its way toward business.

. . . .

We have a tendency to perceive production as a linear process of resource extraction, manufacture and sales, with little or no consideration given to events that occur afterwards.

. . . .

Consumers have a more positive image of a company if they see it doing something to make the world a better place. The future survival of many large brands, therefore, will become increasingly dependent upon both the delivery and perceptibility of environmentally conscious practices and products.

. . . .

Sustainability provides us with the greatest opportunity to radically rethink the way in which we engage with our material worlds; legislation provides the gentle shove that we need to get started.

. . . .

Enabling consumers to develop empathy with the products they own transforms products into talking points, linking consumers to producers though ongoing dialogues.

. . . .

The sentiments of leasing might be better expressed through a deeper after-sales relationship between producer and consumer, which essentially enables the absolute ownership of longer-lasting things.

. . . .

Fostering and maintaining relationships with customers enables businesses to continue generating revenue without the need for further costly manufacturing, resource extraction, energy consumption, atmospheric pollution and waste.

. . . .

If end users have no desire to keep things for longer, they will not. We need to design products that consumers will actually want to keep, maintain and use for longer periods of time.

A toolbox of ideas

Keep up with legislation: maintain currency with legislation so that you can empathize with – and design for – the strict parameters that manufacturers are expected to operate within. Design must endeavour to pioneer new ways to effectively comply with current and forthcoming legislation if it is to serve the needs of a manufacturing industry falling under increasing environmental pressure. Think of environmental legislation as a loose, yet informative, guide to positive change – not the apocalypse to creative freedom itself.

. . . .

Protract engagement: products serve as agents of sustained engagement between producers and users and can, therefore, be seen as the glue that binds. However, this synergy will only manifest itself when users are effectively motivated to keep their things for long periods of time. Increase the richness and longevity of these relationships by creating objects whose slowly unfolding characteristics command deeper, more empathic, modes of material engagement in order to keep users caught in the hook of consuming them.

. . . .

Look beyond the symptoms: be mindful of the cosmetic and largely symptom-focused approach that sustainable design ordinarily adopts. Simply specifying recycled materials, for example, does not equate to sustainable production and consumption. Recycling is a great step in the right direction; but it is imperative that we delve deeper than this if more significant developments are to be made to our grossly inefficient production and consumption cycles.

. . . .

Consider product lifetimes: the designer's role continues throughout an object's entire lifetime, and is about far more than just making things usable, unbreakable and easy on the eye. It is helpful, therefore, to reframe the ongoing interaction between subject and object as a relationship which requires continual growth and evolution if it is to succeed. We as designers must first explore new ways of engendering objects with the capabilities needed to support relationships if this degree of prolonged engagement is, ultimately, to be achieved.

endnotes

Chapter one

1   Burnie, D., *Get a Grip on Ecology*, The Ivy Press, Lewes, 1999, p78
2   Jones, R., *US Insurance Industry Perspectives on Global Climate Change*, Lawrence Berkeley National Laboratory, Berkeley, 2001, p100
3   Lovelock, J., *Gaia: A New Way of Looking at Life on Earth*, Oxford University Press, Oxford, 1995, p43
4   Hardin, G., 'The tragedy of the commons', *Science*, no 162, 1968, pp1243–1248
5   Imberger, J., 'Are we moving towards sustainability?', *Kirby Lecture*, Moore River, Australia, 2003, quoted from www.cwr.uwa.edu.au/presentations/ KirbyLecture/Sustainability_kirby.pdf, September 2003
6   Botting, F. and Wilson, S., *The Bataille Reader*, Blackwell, Oxford, 1997
7   Ibid
8   Ibid
9   UN Population Division, *Population Newsletter*, Department of Economic and Social Affairs, New York, Issue 76, December 2003
10 Ibid
11 US Census Bureau, *Global Population at a Glance: 2002 and Beyond*, US Department of Commerce Economics and Statistics Administration, Washington, DC, March 2004
12 Van Hinte, E. and Bakker, C., *Trespassers: Inspirations for Eco-efficient Design*, The Netherlands Design Institute, Rotterdam, 1999, p23
13 Sessions, G., *Deep Ecology for the 21st Century: Readings on the Philosophy and Practice of the New Environmentalism*, Shambhala, Boston, 1995
14 Hawken, P., Lovins, A. and Hunter Lovins, L., *Natural Capitalism: Creating the Next Industrial Revolution*, Little, Brown and Company, Snowmass, Colorado, 1999, p3
15 Ibid, p2
16 Burnie, D., *Get a Grip on Ecology*, The Ivy Press, Lewes, 1999, p40
17 *ES Magazine*, Associated Newspapers Ltd, 'Put your money where your mouth is', *Evening Standard/ES Magazine*, September 2000
18 *Dow Jones Sustainability Indexes*, quoted from www.sustainability-index. com, May 2002
19 Mont, O., *Functional Thinking: The Role of Functional Sales and Product Service Systems for a Function-Based Society*, International Institute for Industrial Environmental Economics (IIIEE), Lund University, Sweden, no 5233, July 2002, p30
20 *Association of Science – Technology Centers*, quoted from www.astc.org/ exhibitions/rotten/fkl.htm, June 2002

21   Cooper, T., 'Consumers, costs and choice', in Van Hinte, E. (ed) *Eternally Yours: Visions on Product Endurance*, 010 Publishers, Rotterdam, 1997, pp60–61

22   Eternally Yours, *About Eternally Yours*, www.eternally-yours.nl/abouteternally.html, September 2001

23   Thackara, J., 'The design challenge of pervasive computing', *Interactions*, New York, vol 8(3), May/June 2001, pp46–52

24   Manzini, E., 'Ideas of wellbeing: Beyond the rebound effect', *Sustainable Services and Systems: Transitions towards Sustainability*, Amsterdam, 2002

25   Tzu, L., *Tao Te Ching: The Book of the Way*, Kyle Kathie, London, 1988, p122

26   Silverman, H. J., *Derrida and Deconstruction*, Routledge, London, 1989, p85

27   De Groot, C. H., 'Experiencing the Phenomenological Object', *Closing the Gap Between Subject and Object*, Design Transformation Group, London, 1997, pp20–21

28   Dunne, A. and Raby, F., *Design Noir: The Secret Life of Electronic Objects*, Birkhauser, London, 2001, p45

29   Design Transformation Group, *Closing the Gap between Subject and Object*, London, 1997, p20

30   Anderson, L., 'So here are the questions: Is time long or is it wide?', in Van Hinte, E. (ed) *Eternally Yours: Visions on Product Endurance*, 010 Publishers, Rotterdam, 1997, p19

31   Lipps, T., *Academy Lecture*, 209/2, Germany, August 1912

32   Imberger, J., 'Are we moving towards sustainability?', *Kirby Lecture*, Moore River, Australia, 2003, www.cwr.uwa.edu.au/presentations/KirbyLecture/Sustainability_kirby.pdf, September 2003

33   AtKisson, A., *Believing Cassandra: An Optimist Looks at a Pessimist's World*, Chelsea Green, White River Junction, Vermont, 1999

34   Treanor, P., *Why Sustainability Is Wrong*, www.web.inter.nl.net/users/Paul.Treanor/sustainability.html, September 2004

35   Duvall, B., 'The unsustainability of sustainability', *Culture Change Homepage: A Project of the Sustainable Energy Institute*, www.culturechange.org/issue19/unsustainability.htm, September 2004

36   Ibid

37   Manzini, E., cited on the *Eternally Yours* homepage, www.home.wxs.nl/~muis/eternal.htm, April 1997

Chapter two

1   Palahniuk, C., *Fight Club*, Henry Holt and Company Inc, New York, 1999

2   Nitto, N. and Shiozaki, J., 'Changing consumption patterns and new lifestyles in the 21st century', *NRI Papers*, no 24, March 2001, p12

3   Environmental Defence Fund Advertisement, *The Christian Science Monitor*, 1990

4   Carson, R., *Silent Spring*, Houghton Mifflin, Boston, 1962

5   Macpherson, C. B., *Property: Mainstream and Critical Positions*, University of Toronto Press, Toronto, 1978

6   Greenpeace, advertisement that featured in *The New York Times*, 25 February 1990

7   Fromm, E., *To Have or To Be*, Abacus, London, 1979, p11

8   Palahniuk, C., *Fight Club*, Henry Holt and Company Inc, New York, 1999

9   Fuller, T. *Gnomologia, Adagies and Proverbs, Wise Sentences and Witty Sayings, Ancient and Modern, Foreign and British*, Kessinger Publishing, Whitefish, July 2003

10 Wachowski, L. and Wachowski, A., *The Matrix*, Warner Studios, Los Angeles, 1999

11 *Etymology Online*, www.etymonline.com/c8etym.htm, August 2003

12 Schumacher, E. F., *Small Is Beautiful: Economics as if People Mattered*, Harper Perennial, New York, 1989

13 Bocock, R., *Consumption*, Routledge, London, 1993

14 Cupchik, G. C., 'Emotion and industrial design: Reconciling meanings and feelings', *First International Conference on Design and Emotion*, Delft University of Technology, Delft, 1999

15 Palahniuk, C., *Fight Club*, Henry Holt and Company Inc, New York, 1999

16 Buy Nothing Day Organization, www.buynothingday.co.uk, November 1999

17 Kleine, R. E. and Kernan, J. B., 'Measuring the meaning of consumption objects: An empirical investigation', *Advances in Consumer Research*, vol 15, 1988, pp498–504

18 Ibid

19 Fromm, E., *To Have or To Be*, Abacus, London, 1979, p26

20 Ibid

21 Koskijoki, M., 'My favourite things', in Van Hinte, E. (ed) *Eternally Yours: Visions on Product Endurance*, 010 Publishers, Rotterdam, 1997, pp134–135

22 Van Hinte, E., *Eternally Yours: Visions on Product Endurance*, 010 Publishers, , Rotterdam, 1997, p48

23 Yen Mah, A., *Watching the Tree*, Harper Collins, London, 2000

24 Nitto, N. and Shiozaki, J., 'Changing consumption patterns and new lifestyles in the 21st century', *NRI Papers*, no 24, March 2001, p12

25 Ibid, p13

26 Ibid, p12

27 Gould, S. J., 'Our allotted lifetimes', *Natural History*, New York, vol 86/87, 1977, pp34–41

28 White, L., 'The historical roots of our ecological crisis', *Science*, March, vol 155, 1967, pp1203–1207

29 Dubos, R., *The Wooing of Earth*, MacMillan Publishing Company, New York, 1981

30 Lyman, F., *The Greenhouse Trap*, Beacon Press, Boston, 1990

31 Pollan, M., *Second Nature*, Dell Publishing, New York, 1995

32 Feyerabend, P., *Against Method*, Verso, London, 1993

33 Mont, O., *Functional Thinking: The Role of Functional Sales and Product Service Systems for a Function-based Society*, International Institute for Industrial Environmental Economics, Lund University, Sweden, no 5233, July 2002, p30

34 Fromm, E., *To Have or To Be*, Abacus, London, 1979, p27

35 Sartre, J. P., *Being and Nothingness: A Phenomenological Essay on Ontology*, Routledge, London, 1969

36 Gregory, P., 'A four-legged friend', *Digital Home Magazine*, August 2003, p114

37 Leader, D. and Groves, J., *Introducing Lacan*, Icon Books, London, 1995

38 Ibid

39 Freud, S., *Civilization and Its Discontents*, W. W. Norton and Company, New York, 1989

40 Leader, D. and Groves, J., *Introducing Lacan*, Icon Books, London, 1995

41 Ibid

42 Crampton-Smith, G., 'The art of interaction', Paper presented at *Doors3: Info-Eco*, Doors of Perception, The Netherlands Design Institute, Amsterdam, 1993

43 Schopenhauer, A., *On the Vanity of Existence*, Scholarly Press, Michigan, 1970

Chapter three

1 Hyper Dictionary, cited from www.hyperdictionary.com/dictionary/animism, September 2003

2 Mitchell, L., 'Suddenly smarter', *Stanford Magazine*, July/August 2002

3 Ibid

4 Ibid

5 Ibid

6 Ibid

7 Gerasirnov, D. V., *Chronology of Vegetation and Paleoclimatic Stages of Northwestern Russia During the Late Glacial and Holocene*, Institute of History of Material Culture, Russian Academy of Sciences, St Petersburg, 2002

8 Achterhuis, H., 'Equality's safety belt', in Van Hinte, E. (ed) *Eternally Yours: Visions on Product Endurance*, 010 Publishers, Rotterdam, 1997, p82

9 Verbeek, P. P. and Kockelkoren, P., 'Matter matters', in Van Hinte, E. (ed) *Eternally Yours: Visions on Product Endurance*, 010 Publishers, Rotterdam, 1997, p102

10 Ibid, p103

11 Brunner, F. M., *Consumerism and Relationships: The Psychology of Extropersonal Relationships*, cited on www.hooked.net/~brunner, November 1996

12 Ibid

13 Ibid

14 Cushman, P., *Constructing the Self, Constructing America: A Cultural History of Psychotherapy*, Perseus Publishing, Reading, US, 1997

15 Brunner, F. M., *On Consumerism*, cited on www.geocities.com/meifania/consumerism.html, October 2003

16 Ramakers, R., 'Contemporary engagement', in Joris, Y. (ed) *Wanders Wonders: Design for a New Age*, 010 Publishers, Rotterdam, 1999, p7

17 UNDP (United Nations Development Programme), 'The state of human development', *Human Development Report 1998 Overview*, cited on www.hdr.undp.org/reports/global/1998/en/pdf/hdr_1998_overview.pdf, January 2001

18 Shah, A., *Behind Consumption and Consumerism*, cited on Global Issues website, www.globalissues.org/TradeRelated/Consumption.asp, May 2003

19 Searles, H. F., *The Nonhuman Environment*, International University Press, New York, 1960, p30

20   Dunne, A. and Raby, F., *Design Noir: The Secret Life of Electronic Objects*, Birkhauser, London, 2001, p8

21   Gray, J., *Men Are from Mars, Women Are from Venus*, Element/Thorsons, London, 2002, p 293

22   Ibid, p294

23   Brook, T., 'Tony Brook, Spin, on the G5', *Creative Review: Peer Poll 2004*, Creative Review, October 2004, vol 24, no 10, p45

24   Dunne, A. and Raby, F., *Design Noir: The Secret Life of Electronic Objects*, Birkhauser, London, 2001, p8

25   Hummels, C., 'Engaging contexts to evoke experiences', *First International Conference on Design and Emotion*, Delft University of Technology, Delft, The Netherlands, 1999

26   Ibid

27   Dunne, A. and Raby, F., *Design Noir: The Secret Life of Electronic Objects*, Birkhauser, London, 2001, p45

28   Ibid, p8

29   Kusahara, M., 'The art of creating subjective reality: An analysis of Japanese digital pets', *Leonardo*, vol 34, no 4, 2001, p300

30   Ibid, p301

31   Ibid, p301

32   Philips Design, *Visions of the Future*, Philips Design, Eindhoven, 1996, p191

33   Djajadiningrat, T., Overbeeke, K. and Wensveen, S., *But How, Donald, Tell Us How?: On the Creation of Meaning in Interaction Design through Feedforward and Inherent Feedback*, ACM Press, New York, 2001

34   Norman, D., *The Design of Everyday Things*, Basic Books, New York, 2002, p27

35   Van Hinte, E., *Eternally Yours: Visions on Product Endurance*, 010 Publishers, Rotterdam, 1997, p126

36   Ibid, p189

37   Manzini, E., 'Sustainability and scenario building: Scenarios of sustainable wellbeing and sustainable solutions development', *Second International Symposium on Environmentally Conscious Design and Inverse Manufacturing*, EcoDesign'01, Tokyo, 11–15 December 2001.

38   Van Hinte, E., *Eternally Yours: Visions on Product Endurance*, 010 Publishers, Rotterdam, 1997, p188

39   Ramakers, R., 'Contemporary engagement', in Joris, Y. (ed) *Wanders Wonders: Design for a New Age*, 010 Publishers, Rotterdam, 1999, p7

Chapter four

1   Shedroff, N., *Experience Design 1*, New Riders Publishing, Thousand Oaks, 2001

2   Cupchik, G. C., 'Emotion and industrial design: Reconciling meanings and feelings', *First International Conference on Design and Emotion*, Delft University of Technology, Delft, 1999

3   Microsoft Corporation, *Encarta World English Dictionary*, Bloomsbury Publishing Plc, London, 1999

4   Ibid

5   Design and Emotion Society, 'Conference themes', *Design and Emotion 2004*, cited on www.designandemotion.org/de61.php, August 2004

6   Cupchik, G. C., 'Emotion and industrial design: Reconciling meanings and feelings', *First International Conference on Design and Emotion*, Delft University of Technology, Delft, The Netherlands, 1999

7   Science Museum, *Science and Society Picture Library*, cited on www.nmsi.ac.uk/piclib/images/preview/10320850.jpg, August 2004

8   Shedroff, N., *Experience Design*, cited on www.nathan.com/ed/index.html, March 2004

9   Jacobsen, B., 'Experience design', *A List Apart Magazine*, www.alistapart.com/stories/experience, July 2002

10 Ibid

11 Shedroff, N., *Experience Design*, cited on www.nathan.com/ed/index.html, March 2004

12 American Institute of Graphic Arts, cited on www.aiga.org/content.cfm, August 2004

13 Ibid

14 Jacobsen, B., 'Experience Design', *A List Apart Magazine*, www.alistapart.com/stories/experience, July 2002

15 Movius One, *Experience Design*, cited on www.moviusone.com/philosophy_exp_design.html, May 2004

16 DiSalvo, C., Hanington, B. and Forlizzi, J., 'An accessible framework of emotional experiences for new product conception', in McDonagh, D., Hekkert, P., Erp, J. van and Gyi, D. (eds), *Design and Emotion: The Experience of Everyday Things*, Taylor and Francis, London, 2004

17 Design and Emotion Society, 'Conference themes', *Design and Emotion 2004*, cited on www.designandemotion.org/de61.php, August 2004

18 Cupchik, G. C., 'Emotion and industrial design: Reconciling meanings and feelings', *First International Conference on Design and Emotion*, Delft University of Technology, Delft, The Netherlands, 1999

19 Ibid

20 Norman, D., *Emotional Design: Why We Love (or Hate) Everyday Things*, Basic Books, New York, 2004, p7

21 Ibid, p5

22 Ortony, A., Clore, G. L. and Collins, A., *The Cognitive Structure of Emotions*, Cambridge University Press, Cambridge, 1988

23 Design and Emotion Society, 'Conference themes', *Design and Emotion 2004*, cited on www.designandemotion.org/de61.php, August 2004

24 Ibid

25 Cupchik, G. C., 'Emotion and industrial design: Reconciling meanings and feelings', *First International Conference on Design and Emotion*, Delft University of Technology, Delft, The Netherlands, 1999

26 Ibid

27 Ibid

28 Design and Emotion Society, 'Conference themes', *Design and Emotion 2004*, cited on www.designandemotion.org/de61.php, August 2004

29 Microsoft Corporation, *Encarta World English Dictionary*, Bloomsbury Publishing Plc, London, 1999

30 Cupchik, G. C., 'Emotion in aesthetics: Reactive and reflective models', *Poetics*, vol 23, 1995, pp177–188

31 Cupchik, G. C., 'Suspense and disorientation: Two poles of emotionally charged literary uncertainty', in Vorderer, P., Wulff, H. J. and Friedrichsen, M. (eds) *Suspense: Conceptualizations, Theoretical Analyses and Empirical Explorations*, Lawrence Erlbaum Associates, Raleigh, 1996, pp189–197

32 Microsoft Corporation, *Encarta World English Dictionary*, Bloomsbury Publishing Plc, London, 1999

33 Richmond, W., *Design Technology*, cited on www.fredraab.com/careprint2.htm, August 2004

34 Ibid

35 Philips Research, *What Is Ambient Intelligence*, Royal Philips Electronics, 2002, cited on www.research.philips.com/InformationCenter/Global/FArticleSummary.asp, September 2003

36 Edgar Web Design Guide, *Emotional Design*, cited on Edgar Web Design Guide website, www.eserver.org/courses/w01/tc510/edgar/Darryl, August 2004

37 Philips Research, *What Is Ambient Intelligence*, Royal Philips Electronics, 2002, cited on www.research.philips.com/InformationCenter/Global/FArticleSummary.asp, September 2003

38 Philips Research, *Projects Aiming for the 'Immersive Experience'*, Royal Philips Electronics, 2002, cited on www.research.philips.com/InformationCenter/Global/FArticleDetail.asp, August 2003

39 Van Hinte, E., *Eternally Yours: Visions on Product Endurance*, 010 Publishers, 1997, p122

40 De Groot, C. H., *The Consciousness of Objects – Or the Darker Side of Design*, Birmingham Institute of Art and Design, University of Central England, Birmingham, 2002

Chapter five

1 Schultz, S. E., Kleine, R. E. and Kernan, J. B., 'These are a few of my favourite things: Toward an explication of attachment as a consumer behaviour construct', *Advances in Consumer Research*, vol 16, 1989, pp359–366

2 Hybs, I., 'Beyond interface: A phenomenological view of computer systems design', *Leonardo*, vol 23(3), 1996

3 Norman, D., *JND: Just Noticeable Difference*, cited on www.jnd.org/jnd.html, January 2003

4 Gordon, A. and Suzuki, D., *It's a Matter of Survival*, Allen and Unwin, Sydney, 1990

5 Ibid

6 Ibid

7 St. Lukes Advertising Agency, *Sensorama*, cited on www.stlukes.co.uk/standard/senses/index.htm, September 2001

8 Levi Strauss and Co, *A History of Denim*, cited from the Levi Strauss website, www.levistrauss.com/about/history/denim.htm, September 2004

9   Weston Thomas, P., 'Denim jeans', *Fashion Era* website, www.fashion-era. com/denim_jeans_and_casual_wear.htm, September 2004

10   Levi Strauss and Co, *A History of Denim*, cited from the Levi Strauss website, www.levistrauss.com/about/history/denim.htm, September 2004

11   Ibid

12   Bedbury, S., *A New Brand World*, Viking Press, New York, 2002

13   Grinyer, C., *Smart Design: Products that Change Our Lives*, RotoVision, Hove, 2001

14   Schultz, S. E., Kleine, R. E. and Kernan, J. B., 'These are a few of my favourite things: Toward an explication of attachment as a consumer behaviour construct', *Advances in Consumer Research*, vol 16, 1989, pp359–366

15   Design Transformation Group, *Closing the Gap between Subject and Object*, Design Transformation Group, London, 1997

16   Csikszentmihalyi, M. and Rochberg-Halton, E., *The Meaning of Things: Domestic Symbols and the Self*, Cambridge University Press, Cambridge, 1981

17   Schultz, S. E., Kleine, R. E. and Kernan, J. B., 'These are a few of my favourite things: Toward an explication of attachment as a consumer behaviour construct', *Advances in Consumer Research*, vol 16, 1989, pp359-366

18   Gates, J., *The Ownership Solution*, Penguin, London, 1998, p163

19   Sartre, J. P., *Being and Nothingness: A Phenomenological Essay on Ontology*, Routledge, London, 1969

20   Botting, F. and Wilson, S., *The Bataille Reader*, Blackwell, Oxford, 1997

21   De Monchy, M. F., *Powermatics: A Discursive Critique of New Technology*, Routledge, 1987

22   Samp, J., *Extracts from French Journalist Sophie Duroux's Interview with Howard Besser*, 10–12 July 1997, cited on www.gseis.ucla.edu/~howard/ papers/tamagotchi.html, December 1999

23   Schultz, S. E., Kleine, R. E. and Kernan, J. B., 'These are a few of my favourite things: Toward an explication of attachment as a consumer behaviour construct', *Advances in Consumer Research*, vol 16, 1989, pp359–366

24   De Groot, C. H., *The Consciousness of Objects – or the Darker Side of Design*, Birmingham Institute of Art and Design, University of Central England, Birmingham, 2002

25   Shelley, M., *Frankenstein: The Modern Prometheus*, Oxford Paperbacks, Oxford, 1998

26   Aldiss, B. W., *Billion Year Spree: The True History of Science Fiction*, Schocken Books, New York, 1974

27   Woodbridge, K. A., *The 'Birth' of a Monster*, www.kimwoodbridge.com/maryshel/birth.shtml, September 2004

28   Asimov, I., *I, Robot*, Voyager Classics, New York, 2001

29   Seiler, E., 'I, Robot, starring Will Smith', *Asimov Online*, cited on www. asimovonline.com, September 2004

30   Mander, J., *Four Arguments for the Elimination of Television*, Harvester Press, Brighton, 1980

31   Ibid

32 Lasn, K., *Culture Jam: The Uncooling of America*, Eagle Brook, New York, 1999

33 Ibid

34 Dunne, A. and Raby, F., *Design Noir: The Secret Life of Electronic Objects*, Birkhauser, London, 2001, p46

35 Ibid

36 Botting, F. and Wilson, S., *The Bataille Reader*, Blackwell, Oxford, 1997

37 Benyus, J. M., *Biomimicry: Innovation Inspired by Nature*, William Morrow, New York, 1997, p95

38 Van Hinte, E., *Eternally Yours: Visions on Product Endurance*, 010 Publishers, Rotterdam, 1997, p131

39 De Groot, C. H., *Experiencing the Phenomenological Object*, The Design Transformation Group, London, 1997

Chapter six

1 Kleine, J. H., 'An island of socialism in sixteenth century Europe; Socialism in the Utopia of Sir Thomas More', *Introduction to English Literature 110-200*, AHM Publishing Corporation, Illinois, November 20 1993, cited on the Thomas More website, www.d-holliday.com/tmore/socialism.htm, July 2004

2 Rifkin, J., *The End of Work: The Decline of the Global Labor Force and the Dawn of the Post-Market Era*, G. P. Putnam and Sons, New York, 1995, p42

3 Shostak, A. B., *Utopian Thinking in Sociology: Creating the Good Society*, American Sociological Association, Washington, DC, 2001

4 Winer, D., 'Monoculture, an Artifact of the 20th Century?', cited on www.davenet.scripting.com/2002/05/13/monocultureAnArtifactOfThe20thCentury, August 2004

5 Dunne, A. and Raby, F., *Design Noir: The Secret Life Of Electronic Objects*, London, 2001, p59

6 Mitchell, M., *Gone with the Wind*, Macmillan, New York, 1936

7 Dicks, P. K., *Blade Runner: Do Androids Dream of Electric Sheep?* Del Rey Books, New York, 1990

8 Orwell, G., *1984*, Signet Books, re-issue edition, New York, 1990

9 Gibson, W., *Neuromancer*, Voyager, Harper Collins Publishers Ltd, 1995

10 Wood, J., *The Virtual Embodied: Presence/Practice/Technology*, Routledge, London and New York, 1998

11 Dunne, A. and Raby, F., *Design Noir: The Secret Life of Electronic Objects*, Birkhauser, London, 2001, p6

12 Sartre, J. P., *Being and Nothingness: A Phenomenological Essay on Ontology*, Routledge, London, 1969

13 Pearsall, J., *The Oxford Concise English Dictionary*, Oxford University Press, Oxford, 1999

14 Ibid

15 Hybs, I., 'Beyond interface: A phenomenological view of computer systems design', *Leonardo*, vol 23(3), 1996, pp215–223

16 Lasn, K., *Culture Jam: How To Reverse America's Suicidal Consumer Binge – and Why We Must*, Perennial Currents, New York, 2000

17 Van Hinte, E., *Eternally Yours: Visions on Product Endurance*, 010 Publishers, Rotterdam, 1997, p234

18 Benedict, R., *Patterns of Culture*, Routledge and Kegan Paul Ltd, London, 1955, p2

19 Silverman, H. J., *Derrida and Deconstruction*, Routledge, London, 1989, p85

20 Sartre, J. P., *Being and Nothingness: A Phenomenological Essay on Ontology*, Routledge, London, 1969

21 MacKay, D. J. C., *Information Theory, Inference and Learning Algorithms*, Cambridge University Press, Cambridge, 2003

22 Ibid

23 Lynch, D., *Blue Velvet*, De Laurentis, New York, 1986

Chapter seven

1 Joris, Y., *Wanders Wonders: Design for a New Age*, 010 Publishers, Rotterdam, 1999, p16

2 Ramakers, R., 'Contemporary engagement', in Joris, Y. (ed) *Wanders Wonders: Design for a New Age*, 010 Publishers, Rotterdam, 1999, p7

3 Hawken, P., Lovins, A. and Hunter Lovins, L., *Natural Capitalism: Creating the Next Industrial Revolution*, Little, Brown and Company, Snowmass, Colorado, 1999

4 Benyus, J. M., *Biomimicry: Innovation Inspired by Nature*, William Morrow, New York, 1997, p238

5 Ibid, p279

6 *ES Magazine*, Associated Newspapers Ltd, 'Put your money where your mouth is', *Evening Standard/ES Magazine*, September 2000

7 Ibid

8 Cooper, T., 'Consumers, costs and choice', in Van Hinte, E. (ed) *Eternally Yours: Visions on Product Endurance*, 010 Publishers, Rotterdam, 1997, p63

9 Hawken, P., Lovins, A. and Hunter Lovins, L., *Natural Capitalism: Creating the Next Industrial Revolution*, Little, Brown and Company, Snowmass, Colorado, 1999

10 Ibid

11 Van Hinte, E., *Eternally Yours: Visions on Product Endurance*, 010 Publishers, Rotterdam, 1997, p222

12 Design and Emotion Society, 'Conference themes', *Design and Emotion 2004*, cited on www.designandemotion.org/de61.php, August 2004

13 Verbeek, P. P. and Kockelkoren, P., 'Matter matters', in Van Hinte, E. (ed) *Eternally Yours: Visions on Product Endurance*, 010 Publishers, Rotterdam, 1997, p106

14 Hafkamp, W., 'Immaterialization', in Van Hinte, E. (ed) *Eternally Yours: Visions on Product Endurance*, 010 Publishers, Rotterdam, 1997, p43

15 Van Hinte, E., *Eternally Yours: Visions on Product Endurance*, 010 Publishers, Rotterdam, 1997, p27

references

Achterhuis, H., 'Equality's safety belt', in Van Hinte, E. (ed) *Eternally Yours: Visions on Product Endurance*, 010 Publishers, Rotterdam, 1997

Aldiss, B.W., *Billion Year Spree: The True History of Science Fiction*, Schocken Books, New York, 1974

American Institute of Graphic Arts, cited on www.aiga.org/content.cfm, August 2004

Anderson, L., 'So here are the questions: Is time long or is it wide?', in Van Hinte, E. (ed) *Eternally Yours: Visions on Product Endurance*, 010 Publishers, Rotterdam,, 1997

Asimov, I., *I, Robot*, Voyager Classics, New York, 2001

Association of Science – Technology Centers, cited on www.astc.org/exhibitions/rotten/fkl.htm, June 2002

AtKisson, A., *Believing Cassandra: An Optimist Looks at a Pessimist's World*, Chelsea Green, White River Junction, Vermont, 1999

Barthes, R., *Empire of Signs*, Jonathan Cape, New York, 1982

Barthes, R., *Mythologies*, Paladin Books, London, 1973

Baudrillard, J., *Selected Readings*, Polity Press, Cambridge, 1988

Baudrillard, J., *Symbolic Exchange and Death*, Sage Publications, London, 1993

Bedbury, S., *A New Brand World*, Viking Press, New York, 2002

Belk, R. W., *Collecting in a Consumer Society*, Routledge, London and New York, 1995

Benedict, R., *Patterns of Culture*, Routledge and Kegan Paul Ltd, London, 1955

Benyus, J. M., *Biomimicry: Innovation Inspired by Nature*, William Morrow, New York, 1997

Bocock, R., *Consumption*, Routledge, London, 1993

Botting, F. and Wilson, S., *The Bataille Reader*, Blackwell, Oxford, 1997

Breazeal, C., *Designing Sociable Robots*, Cambridge, MA, MIT Press, 2002

Breggin, P. R., Breggin, G. R. and Bemak, F., *Dimensions of Empathic Theory*, first edition Springer, New York, 2001

Brewer, J. and Porter, R., *Consumption and the World of Goods*, Routledge, London, 1994

Brook, T., 'Tony Brook, Spin, on the G5', *Creative Review: Peer Poll 2004*, Creative Review, October 2004, vol 24, no 10

Brunner, Fritz M., *Consumerism and Relationships: The Psychology of Extropersonal Relationships*, cited on www.hooked.net/~brunner, November 1996

Brunner, F. M., *On Consumerism*, cited on www.geocities.com/meifania/consumerism. html, October 2003

Burall, P., *Green Design*, The Design Council, London, 1991

Burnie, D., *Get a Grip on Ecology*, The Ivy Press, Lewes, 1999

Buy Nothing Day Organization, cited on www.buynothingday.co.uk, November 1999

Cacioppo, J. T., *The Psychophysiology of Emotion*, The Guildford Press, New York, 2001

Carson, R., *Silent Spring*, Houghton Mifflin, Boston, 1962

Carter, R. E., *Becoming Bamboo: Western and Eastern Explorations of the Meaning of Life*, McGill-Queens University Press, Kingston and Montreal, 1992

Chomsky, N., *The Prosperous Few and the Restless Many*, Odonian Press, Berkeley, California, 1993

Cooper, T., 'Consumers, costs and choice', in Van Hinte, E. (ed) *Eternally Yours: Visions on Product Endurance*, 010 Publishers, Rotterdam, 1997

Crampton-Smith, G., 'The art of interaction', Paper presented at *Doors3: Info-Eco*, Doors of Perception, The Netherlands Design Institute, Amsterdam, 1993

Crozier, R., *Manufactured Pleasures: Psychological Responses to Design*, Manchester University Press, Manchester, 1994

Csikszentmihalyi, M., *Flow: The Psychology of Optimal Experience*, Harper and Row, New York, 1990

Csikszentmihalyi, M. and Rochberg-Halton, E., 'People and things: Reflections on materialism', *The University of Chicago Magazine*, vol 70(3), Chicago, 1978

Csikszentmihalyi, M. and Rochberg-Halton, E., *The Meaning of Things: Domestic Symbols and the Self*, Cambridge, 1981

Cupchik, G. C., 'Emotion and industrial design: Reconciling meanings and feelings', *First International Conference on Design and Emotion*, Delft University of Technology, Delft, The Netherlands, 1999

Cupchik, G. C., 'Emotion in aesthetics: Reactive and reflective models', *Poetics*, vol 23, 1995

Cupchik, G. C., 'Suspense and disorientation: Two poles of emotionally charged literary uncertainty', in Vorderer, P., Wulff, H. J. and Friedrichsen, M. (eds) *Suspense: Conceptualizations, Theoretical Analyses and Empirical Explorations*, Lawrence Erlbaum Associates, Mahwah, 1996

Cushman, P., *Constructing the Self, Constructing America: A Cultural History of Psychotherapy*, Perseus Publishing, Boston, 1997

Datschefski, E., *The Total Beauty of Sustainable Products*, Rotovision, Hove, 2001

De Groot, C. H., 'Experiencing the phenomenological object', *Closing the Gap between Subject and Object*, Design Transformation Group, London, 1997

De Groot, C. H., *Notes: Changing Energy into Form*, Ellipsis, London, 1999

De Groot, C. H., *The Consciousness of Objects – or the Darker Side of Design*, Birmingham Institute of Art and Design, University of Central England, Birmingham, 2002

De Monchy, M. F., *Powermatics: A Discursive Critique of New Technology*, Routledge, London, 1987

Design and Emotion Society, 'Conference themes', *Design and Emotion 2004*, cited on www.designandemotion.org/de61.php, August 2004

Design Transformation Group, *Closing the Gap between Subject and Object*, Design
    Transformation Group, London, 1997
Dichter, E., *The Strategy of Desire*, Doubleday, New York, 1960
Dicks, P. K., *Blade Runner: Do Androids Dream of Electric Sheep?* Del Rey Books, New
    York, 1990
DiSalvo, C., Hanington, B. and Forlizzi, J., 'An accessible framework of emotional
    experiences for new product conception', in McDonagh, D., Hekkert, P., Erp,
    J. van and Gyi, D. (eds), *Design and Emotion: The Experience of Everyday Things*,
    Taylor and Francis, London, 2004
Dittiner, H., *The Social Psychology of Material Possessions, Harvester and Wheatsheaf*, St
    Martins Press, New York, 1992
Djajadiningrat, T., Overbeeke, K. and Wensveen, S., *But How, Donald, Tell Us How?: On
    the Creation of Meaning in Interaction Design through Feedforward and Inherent
    Feedback*, ACM Press, New York, 2001
Douthwaite, R., *The Growth Illusion*, Green Books, Totness, 1992
Dow Jones Sustainability Indexes, cited on www.sustainability-index.com, May 2002
Dubos, R., *The Wooing of Earth*, MacMillan Publishing Company, New York, 1981
Dunne, A. and Raby, F., *Design Noir: The Secret Life of Electronic Objects*, Birkhauser,
    London, 2001
Duvall, B., 'The unsustainability of sustainability', *Culture Change homepage – A
    project of the Sustainable Energy Institute*, www.culturechange.org/issue19/
    unsustainability.htm, September 2004
Eco, U., *A Theory of Semiotics*, Macmillan, London, 1977
Eco, U., *Art and Beauty in the Middle Ages*, Yale University Press, Newhaven, 1986
Eco, U., *Travels in Hyperreality*, Picador, London, 1986
Edgar Web Design Guide, *Emotional Design*, cited on Edgar Web Design Guide
    website, www.eserver.org/courses/w01/tc510/edgar/Darryl, August 2004
Elrod, J. W., *Being and Existence in Kierkegaard's Pseudonymous Works*, Princeton
    University Press, Princeton, 1975
Environmental Defence Fund Advertisement, *The Christian Science Monitor*,
    Houston, 1990
ES Magazine, Associated Newspapers Ltd, 'Put your money where your mouth is',
    Evening Standard/ES Magazine, September 2000
Eternally Yours, *About Eternally Yours*, www.eternally-yours.nl/abouteternally.html,
    September 2001
Etymology Online, cited on www.etymonline.com/c8etym.htm, August 2003
Evernden, N., *The Natural Alien: Humankind and Environment*, University of Toronto
    Press, Toronto, 1985
Faud-Luke, A., *The Eco-Design Handbook*, Thames and Hudson Ltd, London, 2002
Feyerabend, P., *Against Method*, Verso, London, 1993
Feyerabend, P., *Farewell to Reason*, Verso, New York, 1987
Flusser, V., *The Shape of Things: A Philosophy of Design*, Reaktion Books, London, 1999
Freud, S., *Civilization and Its Discontents*, W. W. Norton and Company, New York, 1989
Fromm, E., *The Art of Being*, Constable, London, 1993
Fromm, E., *To Have or To Be*, Abacus, London, 1979

Fry, T., *New Design Philosophy: An Introduction to Defuturing*, UNSW Press, Sydney, 1999

Fry, T., *Remakings*, Envirobook, Sydney, 1994

Fuller, T., *Gnomologia, Adagies and Proverbs, Wise Sentences and Witty Sayings, Ancient and Modern, Foreign and British*, Kessinger Publishing, Whitefish, July 2003

Gates, J., *The Ownership Solution*, Penguin, London, 1998

Gerasirnov, D. V., *Chronology of Vegetation and Paleoclimatic Stages of Northwestern Russia During the Late Glacial and Holocene*, Institute of History of Material Culture, Russian Academy of Sciences, St Petersburg, 2002

Gibson, W., *Neuromancer, Voyager*, Harper Collins Publishers Ltd, London, 1995

Goffman, E., *The Presentation of Self in Everyday Life*, Doubleday and Company, New York, 1959

Goodin, R., *Green Political Theory*, Polity Press, Cambridge, 1992

Gordon, A. and Suzuki, D., *It's a Matter of Survival*, Allen and Unwin, Sydney, 1990

Gould, S. J., 'Our allotted lifetimes', *Natural History*, New York, US, vol 86/7, 1977

Gray, J., *Men Are from Mars, Women Are from Venus*, Element/Thorsons, London, 2002

Greenhalgh, P., *Modernism in Design*, Reaktion Books, London, 1990

Greenpeace, advertisement that featured in *The New York Times*, 25 February, 1990

Gregory, P., 'A four-legged friend', *Digital Home Magazine*, August 2003

Grinyer, C., *Smart Design: Products That Change Our Lives*, RotoVision, Hove, 2001

Guyer, P., *Kant and the Claims of Taste*, Cambridge University Press, Cambridge, 1997

Hafkamp, W., 'Immaterialization', in Van Hinte, E. (ed) *Eternally Yours: Visions on Product Endurance*, 010 Publishers, Rotterdam, 1997

Hardin, G., 'The tragedy of the commons', *Science*, no 162, 1968

Hawken, P., *The Ecology of Commerce*, Phoenix, London, 1994

Hawken, P., Lovins, A. and Hunter Lovins, L., *Natural Capitalism: Creating the Next Industrial Revolution*, Little, Brown and Company, Snowmass, 1999

Hegel, G. W. F., *The Phenomenology of Spirit*, Oxford University Press, Oxford, 1977

Heidegger, M., *Being and Time*, Blackwell, Oxford, 1967

Hobson, M., *Jacques Derrida: Opening Lines*, Routledge, London, 1998

Hummels, C., 'Engaging contexts to evoke experiences', *First International Conference on Design and Emotion*, Delft University of Technology, Delft, 1999

Hybs, I., 'Beyond interface: A phenomenological view of computer systems design', *Leonardo*, volume 23(3), 1996

Hyper Dictionary, cited on www.hyperdictionary.com/dictionary/animism, September 2003

Illich, I., *Energy and Equity*, Marion Boyars, London, 1974

Imberger, J., 'Are we moving towards sustainability?' *Kirby Lecture*, Moore River, Australia, 2003, cited on www.cwr.uwa.edu.au/presentations/KirbyLecture/Sustainability_kirby.pdf, September 2003

Jacobsen, B., 'Experience design', *A List Apart Magazine*, www.alistapart.com/stories/experience, July 2002

Jones, R., *US Insurance Industry Perspectives on Global Climate Change*, Lawrence Berkeley National Laboratory, Berkeley, 2001

Jordan, P. W., *Designing Pleasurable Products: An Introduction to the New Human Factors*, Taylor and Francis, London, 2000

Joris, Y., *Wanders Wonders: Design for a New Age*, 010 Publishers, Rotterdam, 1999

Jung, C. G., *Psychological Reflections*, Oxford University Press, New York, 1987

Klein, N., *No Logo*, Harper Collins, London, 2000

Kleine, J. H., 'An island of socialism in sixteenth century Europe; Socialism in the Utopia of Sir Thomas More', *Introduction to English Literature 110-200*, AHM Publishing Corporation, Illinois, 20 November, 1993, cited on Thomas More website, www.d-holliday.com/tmore/socialism.htm, July 2004

Kleine, R. E. and Kernan, J. B., 'Measuring the meaning of consumption objects: An empirical investigation', *Advances in Consumer Research*, vol 15, 1988, pp498–504

Koskijoki, M., 'My favourite things', in Van Hinte, E. (ed) *Eternally Yours: Visions on Product Endurance*, 010 Publishers, Rotterdam, 1997

Kunkel, P., *Digital Dreams: The Work of the Sony Design Center*, Laurence King Publishing, London, 1999

Kusahara, M., 'The art of creating subjective reality: An analysis of Japanese digital pets', *Leonardo*, vol 34, no 4, 2001, pp299–302

Lasn, K., *Culture Jam: How To Reverse America's Suicidal Consumer Binge – and Why We Must*, Perennial Currents, New York, 2000

Lasn, K., *Culture Jam: The Uncooling of America*, Eagle Brook, New York, 1999

Laurel, B., *The Art of Human–Computer Interface Design*, Addison-Wesley, Reading, MA, 1990

Leader, D. and Groves, J., *Introducing Lacan*, Icon Books, London, 1995

Levi Strauss and Co, *A History of Denim*, www.levistrauss.com/about/history/denim.htm, September 2004

Lipps, T., *Academy Lecture*, 209/2, Germany, August 1912

Lovelock, J., *Healing Gaia*, Gaia Books, London, 1991

Lovelock, J., *Gaia: A New Way of Looking at Life on Earth*, Oxford University Press, Oxford, 1995

Lury, C., *Consumer Culture*, Polity Press, Cambridge, 1996

Lyman, F., *The Greenhouse Trap*, Beacon Press, Boston, 1990

Lynch, D., *Blue Velvet*, De Laurentis, New York, 1986

Macauley, D., *Minding Nature: The Philosophers of Ecology*, Guilford Press, New York, 1996

MacKay, D. J. C., *Information Theory, Inference and Learning Algorithms*, Cambridge University Press, Cambridge, 2003

MacKenzie, D., *Design for the Environment*, Rizzoli, New York, 1991

Macpherson, C. B., *The Political Theory of Possessive Individualism: Hobbes to Locke*, Oxford University Press, London and New York, 1964

Macpherson, C. B., *Property: Mainstream and Critical Positions*, University of Toronto Press, Toronto, 1978

Mander, J., *Four Arguments for the Elimination of Television*, Harvester Press, Brighton, 1980

Mannheim, K., *Ideology and Utopia*, Routledge and Kegan Paul, London, 1963

Manzini, E., cited on *Eternally Yours* homepage, www.home.wxs.nl/~muis/eternal.htm, April 1997

Manzini, E., 'Ideas of wellbeing: Beyond the rebound effect', *Sustainable Services and Systems: Transitions towards Sustainability*, Amsterdam, The Netherlands, 2002

Manzini, E., 'Sustainability and scenario building: Scenarios of sustainable wellbeing and sustainable solutions development', *Second International Symposium on Environmentally Conscious Design and Inverse Manufacturing*, EcoDesign'01, Tokyo, 11–15 December 2001

Manzini, E., *The Material of Invention*, Arcadia, Milan, 1986

Margolin, V., *Design Discourse*, University of Chicago Press, Chicago, 1989

McKenzie, D., *Green Design*, Lawrence Kingsley, London, 1997

McWhorter, L. (ed), *Heidegger and the Earth: Essays in Environmental Philosophy*, Thomas Jefferson University Press, Princeton, 1992

Microsoft Corporation, *Encarta World English Dictionary*, Bloomsbury Publishing Plc, London, 1999

Miller, D., *Material Culture and Mass Consumption*, Blackwell, Oxford, 1991

Mitchell, L., 'Suddenly smarter', *Stanford Magazine*, July/August 2002

Mitchell, M., *Gone With the Wind*, Macmillan, New York, 1936

Mont, O., *Functional Thinking: The Role of Functional Sales and Product Service Systems for a Function-Based Society*, International Institute for Industrial Environmental Economics (IIIEE), Lund University, no 5233, July 2002

Movius One, *Experience Design*, cited on www.moviusone.com/philosophy_exp_design.html, May 2004

Myerson, J., *IDEO: Masters of Innovation*, Laurence King Publishing, London, 2001

Nitto, N. and Shiozaki, J., 'Changing consumption patterns and new lifestyles in the 21st century', *NRI Papers*, Japan, no 24, March 2001

Norman, D., *Emotional Design: Why We Love (or Hate) Everyday Things*, Basic Books, New York, 2004

Norman, D., *JND: Just Noticeable Difference*, cited on www.jnd.org/jnd.html, January 2003

Norman, D., *The Design of Everyday Things*, Basic Books, New York, 2002

Oelschlaeger, M., *The Idea of Wilderness*, Yale University Press, New Haven, 1991

Ortony, A., Clore, G. L. and Collins, A., *The Cognitive Structure of Emotions*, Cambridge University Press, Cambridge, 1988

Orwell, G., *1984*, Signet Books, re-issue edition, New York, 1990

Packard, V., *The Waste Makers*, Penguin, Middlesex, 1963

Packard, V., *The Hidden Persuaders*, Penguin, London, 1981

Palahniuk, C., *Fight Club*, Henry Holt and Company Inc, New York, 1999

Papanek V., *Design for the Real World: Human Ecology and Social Change*, Thames and Hudson, London, 1992

Papanek V., *Design for Human Scale*, Van Nortrand Reinhold Co, New York, 1983

Papanek, V., *The Green Imperative: Natural Design for the Real World*, Thames and Hudson, New York, 1995

Pearsall, J., *The Oxford Concise English Dictionary*, Oxford University Press, Oxford, 1999

Pepper, D., *The Roots of Environmentalism*, Routledge, London and New York, 1984

Philips Design, *Visions of the Future*, Philips Design, Eindhoven, 1996

Philips Research, *Projects Aiming for the 'Immersive Experience'*, Royal Philips Electronics, 2002, cited on www.research.philips.com/InformationCenter/Global/FArticleDetail.asp, August 2003

Philips Research, *What Is Ambient Intelligence*, Royal Philips Electronics, 2002, cited on www.research.philips.com/InformationCenter/Global/FArticleSummary.asp, September 2003

Pollan, M., *Second Nature*, Dell Publishing, New York, 1995

Ponting, C., *A Green History of the World*, Penguin, New York, 1991

Ramakers, R., 'Contemporary engagement', in Joris, Y. (ed) *Wanders Wonders: Design for a New Age*, 010 Publishers, Rotterdam, 1999

Richmond, W., *Design Technology*, cited on www.fredraab.com/careprint2.htm, August, 2004

Rifkin, J., *The End of Work: The Decline of the Global Labor Force and the Dawn of the Post-Market Era*, G. P. Putnam and Sons, New York, 1995

Ryle, G., *The Concept of Mind*, Hutcheson, London, 1949

Samp, J., *Extracts from French Journalist Sophie Duroux's Interview with Howard Besser*, 10–12 July 1997, cited on www.gseis.ucla.edu/~howard/papers/tamagotchi.html, December 1999

Sartre, J. P., *Being and Nothingness: A Phenomenological Essay on Ontology*, Routledge, London, 1969

Sartre, J. P., *Existentialism and Humanism*, Methuen, Sydney, 1973

Sarup, M., *An Introductory Guide to Post-Structuralism and Postmodernism*, Harvester Wheatsheaf, London, 1993

Sassen, S., 'The urban complex in a world economy', *International Social Science Journal*, vol 46, no 1, February 1994, pp43–62

Schama, S., *The Embarrassment of Riches: An Interpretation of Dutch Culture in the Golden Age*, Fontana, London, 1988

Schopenhauer, A., *On the Vanity of Existence*, Scholarly Press, Michigan, 1970

Schultz, S. E., Kleine, R. E. and Kernan, J. B., 'These are a few of my favourite things: Toward an explication of attachment as a consumer behaviour construct', *Advances in Consumer Research*, vol 16, 1989, pp359–366

Schumacher, E. F., *Small Is Beautiful: Economics as if People Mattered*, Harper Perennial, New York, 1989

Science Museum, *Science and Society Picture Library*, cited on www.nmsi.ac.uk/piclib/images/preview/10320850.jpg, August 2004

Searles, H. F., *The Nonhuman Environment*, International University Press, New York, 1960

Seiler, E., 'I, Robot, starring Will Smith', *Asimov Online*, cited on www.asimovonline.com, September 2004

Sessions, G., *Deep Ecology for the 21st Century: Readings on the Philosophy and Practice of the New Environmentalism*, Shambhala, Boston, 1995

Shah, A., *Behind Consumption and Consumerism*, cited on Global Issues website, www.globalissues.org/TradeRelated/Consumption.asp, May 2003

Shedroff, N., *Experience Design*, cited on www.nathan.com/ed/index.html, March 2004

Shedroff, N., *Experience Design 1*, New Riders Publishing, Thousand Oaks, 2001

Shelley, M., *Frankenstein: The Modern Prometheus*, Oxford Paperbacks, Oxford, 1998

Shostak, A. B., *Utopian Thinking in Sociology: Creating the Good Society*, American Sociological Association, Washington, DC, 2001

Silverman, H. J., *Derrida and Deconstruction*, Routledge, London, 1989

Soper, K., *What Is Nature? Culture, Politics and the Non-Human*, Blackwell, Cambridge, MA, 1995

St. Lukes Advertising Agency, *Sensorama*, cited on www.stlukes.co.uk/standard/senses/index.htm, September 2001

Stoodley, B. H., *Concepts of Sigmund Freud*, The Free Press, New York, 1959

Thackara, J., *Design after Modernism*, Thames and Hudson, London, 1988

Thackara, J., 'The design challenge of pervasive computing', *Interactions*, ACM Press, New York, vol 8(3), May/June 2001, pp46–52

Treanor, P., *Why Sustainability Is Wrong*, cited on www.web.inter.nl.net/users/Paul.Treanor/sustainability.html, September 2004

Tymieniecka, A. T. (ed), *Phenomenology of Man and the Human Condition*, Dordrecht, Reidel, 1983

Tzu, L., *Tao Te Ching: The Book of the Way*, Kyle Kathie, London, 1988

UN Population Division, *Population Newsletter*, Department of Economic and Social Affairs, New York, issue 76, December 2003

Underhill, P., *Why We Buy: The Science of Shopping*, Simon and Schuster, New York, 1999

UNDP (United Nations Development Programme) 'The state of human development', *Human Development Report 1998 Overview*, cited on www.hdr.undp.org/reports/global/1998/en/pdf/hdr_1998_overview.pdf, January 2001

US Census Bureau, *Global Population at a Glance: 2002 and Beyond*, US Department of Commerce Economics and Statistics Administration, Washington, DC, March 2004

Van Hinte, E., *Eternally Yours: Visions on Product Endurance*, 010 Publishers, Rotterdam, 1997

Van Hinte, E. and Bakker, C., *Trespassers: Inspirations for Eco-Efficient Design*, The Netherlands Design Institute, Rotterdam, 1999

Verbeek, P. P. and Kockelkoren, P., 'Matter matters', in Van Hinte, E. (ed) *Eternally Yours: Visions on Product Endurance*, 010 Publishers, Rotterdam, 1997

Wachowski, L. and Wachowski, A., *The Matrix*, Warner Studios, Los Angeles, 1999

Wahl, J., *Philosophies of Existence*, Routledge and Kegan Paul, London, 1969

Warnock, M., *Imagination*, Faber and Faber, London, 1976

Weston Thomas, P., 'Denim jeans', *Fashion Era*, www.fashion-era.com/denim_jeans_and_casual_wear.htm, September 2004

White, L., *Medieval Technology and Social Change*, Oxford University Press, Oxford, 1962

White, L., 'The historical roots of our ecological crisis', *Science*, vol 155, March 1967, pp1203–1207

Whitely, N., *Design for Society*, Reaktion Books, London, 1992

Williams, R., *Problems in Materialism and Culture*, Verso, London, 1980

Winer, D., 'Monoculture, an artifact of the 20th century?', cited on www.davenet.scripting.com/2002/05/13/monocultureAnArtifactOfThe20thCentury, August 2004

Wood, J., *The Virtual Embodied: Presence/Practice/Technology*, Routledge, London and New York, 1998

Wood, J. and Taiwo, O., 'Some proprioceptive experiences of being-with', *Problems of Observation and Action Conference*, Amsterdam, 1997

Woodbridge, K. A., *The 'Birth' of a Monster*, www.kimwoodbridge.com/maryshel/birth.shtml, September 2004

Yen Mah, A., *Watching the Tree*, Harper Collins, London, 2000

Zimmerman, D. W., *Metaphysics: The Big Questions*, Blackwell Publishers, London, 1998

Zimmerman, M., *Heidegger's Confrontation with Modernity*, Indiana University Press, Indiana, 1990

index